15·14

The Complete Book of
SPICES

The Complete Book of
SPICES
JILL NORMAN

DORLING KINDERSLEY - LONDON

A DORLING KINDERSLEY BOOK

For Paul, Sasha and Elinor, and for Elizabeth, with love.

Senior editor
Carolyn Ryden

Project editor
Tanya Hines

Art editor
Sarah Scrutton

Designer
Karen Ward

Managing editor
Daphne Razazan

Art director
Anne-Marie Bulat

Photography
Martin Norris

First published in Great Britain in 1990 by
Dorling Kindersley Limited,
9 Henrietta Street, London WC2E 8PS

British Library Cataloguing in Publication Data
Norman, Jill
    The complete book of spices
    1. Spices
    1. Title
    641.3383

    ISBN 0-86318-487-1

Typeset by Bookworm Typesetting, Manchester
Colour reproduction by Chroma Graphics, Singapore
Printed and bound in West Germany by Mohndruck GmbH, Gütersloh

Contents

Introduction

" Ah, que j'aime t'ouvrir cher tiroir aux épices,
Souffle d'Orient gratis, voyage inespéré,
Colombo et Ceylon aux magiques caprices,
A défaut de vous voir, je puis vous respirer."

Roger Lecuyer

What is a spice?

Defined in the *Oxford English Dictionary* as "one or other of various strongly flavoured or aromatic substances of vegetable origin, obtained from tropical plants, commonly used as condiments", spices are aromatic dried roots, bark, buds, seeds, berries and other fruits. The word "spice" derives from the Latin word *species*, meaning specific kind, and later, goods or merchandise.

Most of the important spice plants - cinnamon, pepper, ginger, cloves, nutmeg - are native to the Asian tropics; allspice, vanilla and chillies come from the West Indies and Central America; the Mediterranean basin has produced many of the aromatic seeds - coriander, fenugreek, fennel, poppy, mustard; the colder regions have contributed caraway, dill and juniper.

What makes a spice spicy?

Spices acquire their characteristic odour from volatile constituents in the plant material. These aroma constituents are extracted in steam and are present in the essential oil (a term derived from the word "quintessence" - the embodiment of the specific aroma and flavour) distilled from the plant. The volatile oils are largely responsible for a spice's characteristic flavour, although the pungent principle - the hot sensation produced in the mouth by constituents of spices such as pepper, chillies or ginger - also contributes to flavour. Four specific tastes can be detected in different parts of the mouth - sweet, sour, salty and bitter; pungency can be recognized in taste too, but the rest of the complex flavours of any food or drink are identified through smell.

Our vocabulary for describing smell and taste is extremely poor; they are usually described only in terms of other smells and tastes. "Aromatic" and "pungent" are the two adjectives most used about spices, but in a discussion of several spices, aroma and pungency need to be more accurately defined to make comparisons possible. For example, one group of spices has a distinct anise note: dill, fennel, anise, caraway; cumin and star anise. All are members of the same family except star anise. The anise element in dill is mild and subtle; in fennel it is more clear and distinct; anise itself has a sweetish taste with a note of liquorice; in caraway the anise flavour is more subdued again, although the overall effect is warm and slightly bitter; cumin is the most forceful of the group, its anise tones combine with other constituents to give an acrid, intense character. Star anise often has a more pronounced anise aroma than any of the others; it has sweet and bitter tones and is very liquorice-like. Only a tasting comparison will fix the subtle differences in flavour and aroma levels.

The changing role of spices

Spices were once one of the most expensive items in household accounts and were usually kept locked up in the drawers or compartments of special spice cupboards or boxes. In ancient times they were significant as medicines, preservatives and perfumes. Cassia, ginger and pepper were imported by the Greeks; anise, coriander seeds, saffron and poppy seeds were grown locally, as were thyme, mint and marjoram. Dioscorides' *De Materia Medica*, written in the first century AD, was the earliest Western herbal to describe these plants and remedies based upon them. The Romans were the first to use great quantities of spices in cooking, where they were employed in the same generous manner as they were strewn or burned in houses to drive out noxious smells.

Spices were also popular in the new Islamic empire of Mohammed which reached great cultural heights while western Europe went through the Dark Ages. The court of the Caliphs of Baghdad was renowned for science and medicine, art and poetry, and for its sumptuous banquets. The cooks sought to achieve a harmony of flavours, sweet and sour, aromatic and pungent, using many spices and flavourings from the Orient and Middle East such as galangal, cloves, cardamom, nutmeg, cinnamon, pepper, asafoetida, ginger, saffron and rose water.

The widespread use of spices for cooking did not come to Europe until the late Middle Ages. At the end of the 14th century a Parisian housewife could buy spiced sauces from professional saucemakers: "a quart of cameline for the dinner and for the supper two quarts of mustard" were required for a wedding feast, according to *Le Ménagier de Paris* (1393). Made with cinnamon, ginger, cloves, grains of paradise, mace, long pepper, and bread soaked in vinegar, cameline was the most popular sauce of the time. Heavily spiced food remained the norm for the banquets of the rich until the 17th century. Meat and fish were sauced with cinnamon, pepper, cloves, nutmeg, ginger, galangal and saffron throughout Europe. Most dishes were liberally dosed with sugar, sometimes vinegar too, creating a sweet-sour taste. The Germans also used caraway, cumin and lovage seeds; the Italians, fennel.

By the 17th century spices were cheaper and more widely available so they were used with less ostentation by the rich. In baking and sweet dishes they were still important: custards were spiced with nutmeg and cinnamon; saffron cake and seedcake recipes were common. Some of the medieval spices - grains of paradise, cubebs, zedoary - disappeared, but new aromatics arrived from the Americas: allspice, capsicums and vanilla. At the end of the 18th century liquid pickles were on sale as bottled sauces in England. Spices, garlic and fruits were put in casks with vinegar and soy sauce and left to macerate for up to two years. Households and commercial producers had their individual formulae. Among the earliest successful commercial sauces were Lazenby's anchovy essence and Harvey's sauce. Tabasco sauce from Louisiana appeared later in the mid-19th century when Edward McIlhenny, a banker during the Civil War, turned to making sauces.

Today spices are an accepted part of our daily lives. We can choose from a wider selection of spices than we have ever known; try dozens of sauces and essences from all over the world; buy our spices whole or ground, plain or blended as barbecue mix or more dubious-sounding confections such as chicken seasoning, Season-All or Bon Appétit. The increasing choice implies a much deserved revival of interest in spices. Experiment with their flavours and discover their different qualities. Let your palate be the judge of the role spices play in your cooking today.

Jill Norman

1

The spice trade past & present

Spices have been used for thousands of years throughout Asia, Arabia and the Mediterranean region. Once valued as highly as gold, they were much sought after in the West and the quest for spices influenced the course of history dramatically. Countries vied to win control over their production, navigators set sail to discover new sea routes to the East, which eventually allowed small nations to build large empires. Although the days of warring over spices are now over, spices still play a significant role in the economies of many countries.

The origins of the spice trade

Pepper *The spice that inspired the search for new routes to the East and changed the course of history.*

Camel caravan *For centuries spices were transported across Asia from China to Europe along ancient caravan trails such as the Silk Road.*

THE PEOPLES OF the Mediterranean traded for spices from the earliest times. The Egyptians used herbs and spices for embalming, for body ointments and anointing oils, and to fumigate their homes. The Ebers papyrus, a medical document of about 1550 BC, records that anise, caraway, cassia, cardamom, mustard, sesame, fenugreek, saffron and other aromatics were all used by the Egyptians. Frankincense, a resin from trees that grow in the Arabian peninsula, myrrh from East Africa, spices and precious stones from the Far East were taken overland by donkey and later by camel caravans along the Incense Route. This trail led from Hadhramaut in South Arabia along the Arabian coast, then north via Mecca to Egypt and Syria.

Spices are frequently mentioned in the Bible as a valuable commodity; the Queen of Sheba rushed to present Solomon with gold, jewels and spices when through an alliance with his Phoenician neighbours their ships entered the Red Sea, threatening the trade routes she controlled (*Kings* I:10 and *Chronicles* II:9), and Joseph was sold by his brothers to merchants from Gilead travelling to Egypt "with their camels bearing spicery and balm and myrrh" (*Genesis* 37:25). For centuries Arabs acted as middlemen in the trade with the Orient and Africa south of the Sahara. They were in an excellent location, and to preserve their monopoly they kept secret from their Mediterranean customers the provenance of their wares. Alarming tales about the location of spices were put about to discourage the spice buyers from trying to determine the true source of supply and dealing direct.

The Phoenicians distributed spices around the Mediterranean until Tyre, their great commercial centre, fell to Alexander the Great in 332 BC. In the same year he founded Alexandria, the city that was to become the meeting place for merchants from East and West. Several routes were used by the Greeks to bring spices from the East. The oldest sea route was probably that from the Malabar coast of India, up the Persian Gulf and then either via the Tigris and Euphrates valleys to Babylon and Antioch, or round the coast of Arabia and up the Red Sea.

The spice trade in Roman times

The Romans started sailing to India from Egypt in the first century AD; it was a hazardous business and the voyage took two years, until the middle of the century when Hippalus, a Greek merchant sailor, discovered the monsoon winds. Ships sailed to India with the southwest monsoons from April to October and returned with the northeast monsoons blowing from October to April. The journey now took less than a year; the Romans brought back fabulous cargoes and rapidly became extravagant users of spices for perfume, cosmetics, medicine and cooking.

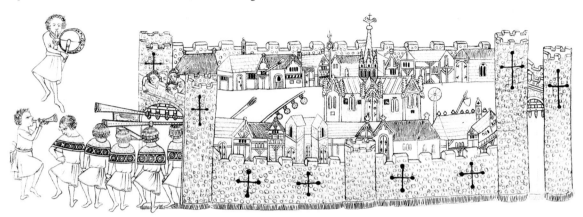

At about the same time the overland route from China, the Silk Road, came into use. Starting from the Chinese city of Chang'an (Xian) it led west, skirting the Himalayas, then on across Persia and the Fertile Crescent to the Mediterranean, or down the Indus valley to the coast, or sometimes north via the Aral and Caspian seas to the Black Sea and Byzantium. The routes varied according to political stability and the taxes levied on caravans, but by the second century the Han emperors extended their control of central Asia far enough to police the roads, and merchants then travelled regularly and in relative safety, carrying silks, jewels, cassia, cumin and ginger to Rome. These land and sea routes continued in use for centuries; indeed the monsoons governed all sea transport to and from India until steamships were introduced.

Constantinople *Once the eastern capital of the Roman empire, the city of Constantinople was the centre for spice trading between East and West.*

Pepper was the most popular Oriental spice in Rome, followed by ginger and turmeric. Most of the recipes in Apicius' *De Re Coquinaria* - "On Cookery" written in the first century AD - included an extensive range of spices to aid digestion, to preserve food and to enhance its flavour. As the Roman empire extended across the Alps the inhabitants of northern Europe acquired the taste for spices too. By the time the Goths laid siege to the city in AD 408 they knew well the value of pepper, silks, gold and silver, and the Romans handed over a huge tribute to prevent the sacking of their city. Rome's fall two years later virtually marked the end of the western empire. Constantinople became the capital of the eastern empire and trade routes developed around the growing city. At about this time too, cloves and nutmegs found their way to the West, probably taken first to India by Indonesian merchants.

The Middle Ages

The flow of goods from East to West dwindled and by the time the Arabs conquered Alexandria in AD 641 it had virtually stopped altogether. The seventh century saw the rise of Islam and by the middle of the eighth century the Arab empire spread from Spain to the borders of China. For 400 years very few spices reached Europe; there was little direct trade between the Muslim Arabs and Christian Europe. In the political and commercial chaos of the Dark Ages which resulted from the barbarian invasions, Europe had nothing to offer in exchange for goods from Asia. The few spices that did arrive were found only in the great houses and palaces and in monasteries and cathedral priories.

Cardamom *Carried to Europe along the ancient caravan routes, cardamom was used medicinally and as a flavouring for centuries in the East.*

Towards the end of his reign Charlemagne decreed that certain herbs and temperate spices, some 70-odd in all, were to be cultivated on all the imperial estates. Monastery gardens were the other places where herbs and spices were grown; the plan of St Gall, made at about the same time, shows a physic garden with beds for cumin, fenugreek, fennel, lovage, mint, rosemary, rue and sage, and a kitchen garden which included celery, coriander, dill, nigella, garlic and poppy.

Monastery accounts give some idea of the spices used in Britain in the Middle Ages; at Norwich cathedral priory in the years 1346 to 1350, purchases of fennel, ginger, galangal, saffron, garlic, pepper, cloves and cubebs were recorded. About 100 years later accounts from Canterbury show expenditure on cloves, mace and saffron. Pepper and other spices were often used as part payment for rents too; mustard is shown as being part of the revenue for lands owned by St Germain-des-Prés in Paris in the 14th century. Spices were taxed at every opportunity; in the tenth century the Statutes of Ethelred required Easterlings (merchants from the Hanseatic towns) to pay 10 lb of pepper as part of a tribute to allow them to trade in London. In 1305 a toll was created to pay for repairs to London Bridge; anise, liquorice and cubebs were among the items taxed. The counts of Provence levied taxes on pepper, ginger, cubebs, cloves, saffron, cumin and sugar from the towns in their domain.

The early European spice trade centres

Trade with the East was reopened by the Crusades in the 11th century. For 200 years there was a stream of Crusaders and pilgrims to the Holy Land where they developed a taste for the foods of that warm climate. Venice and Genoa became principal suppliers to the Crusaders and set up trading concessions in the Near East. Wool, clothing, iron and lumber were exchanged for dates, figs, lemons, oranges, almonds and Oriental spices - pepper, nutmeg and mace, cinnamon, cloves and cardamom. Although spices were still expensive, their use was not restricted to the very wealthy or privileged now, but spread to the middle class. However, the trade was not as easy and natural as it is sometimes made out to be; there were many transactions to be negotiated. A consignment of spices passed through a chain of hands from leaving Aleppo or Alexandria before it reached Lyons or Nürnberg or Bruges. Prices, and sometimes adulteration - although severe penalties were imposed for this crime - increased on each occasion. The Italian city states grew enormously in prosperity and the bitter rivalry between them lasted until Venice defeated Genoa in 1380 and thereafter controlled trade with the Orient for more than 100 years. The Republic enjoyed an unprecedented boom in trade; the demand from Europe for spices, silks and precious stones could probably not have been satisfied had the Indians and Chinese not wanted large quantities of gold, silver, coral, saffron and wool in return.

New routes East and the rise of Portugal

The first steps towards the discovery of new routes to the East were taken in 1418 when Prince Henry (the Navigator) of Portugal set up a navigational school at Sagres in southwest Portugal. He sent out expeditions down the west coast of Africa, hoping to find a route to the East. During his lifetime the Portuguese did not succeed in getting there, but they brought back valuable cargoes from tropical Africa, including grains of paradise.

In May 1498, after a voyage of ten months, the Portuguese explorer Vasco da Gama reached Calicut, the most important port on the west coast of India. After a stay of several months he returned to Portugal with a cargo of spices and jewels, and the news that the ruler was willing to trade with Manuel I. In 1500 Cabral followed with a larger fleet - discovered and took possession of Brazil for Portugal on the way - and a year later returned with a cargo of pepper and other spices. The Venetian monopoly was broken; prices fluctuated wildly; in 1504 Manuel declared a fixed price for pepper and in 1506 made the Lisbon spice trade a crown monopoly.

Vasco da Gama *The Portuguese explorer who discovered the sea route to India via the Cape of Good Hope.*

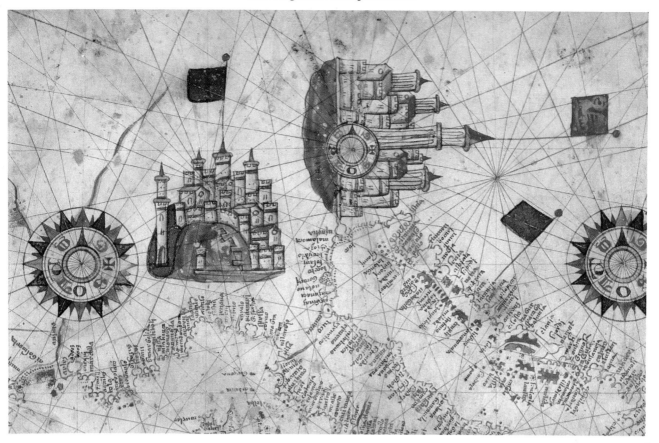

Control of the Spice Islands

By 1510, after battles with the Arabs who for centuries had controlled trade in the Indian Ocean, the Portuguese were established at Goa and on the island of Ceylon. Here they rapidly exploited the cinnamon forests, enslaved the workers and built up a lucrative trade monopoly that was to last well into the 17th century. They moved further east and settled in the trading town of Malacca at the southern end of the Malay peninsula, close to the Spice Islands (the Moluccas) where their cargoes of spices, silks and porcelain were assembled. In due course they moved in to occupy some of the islands too, building fortresses, signing treaties with the local rulers, and oppressing the natives. When the remnants of Magellan's fleet, sailing westwards round the globe under the auspices of the Spanish crown, arrived in the Moluccas in 1522, this set up a struggle between the two powers in the islands until they were united under a common (Spanish) crown in 1580.

The Portuguese were concerned about territorial acquisitions, and to some extent about spreading Catholicism, as well as about trade. Their style of trading was still of the old order; officials were required to provide an annual revenue for the crown, but were also permitted to trade on their own account. The crown tried to restrict local trading by fixing prices and forcing buyers to hand over a percentage of the goods purchased. Not surprisingly the state ended up with the poorer quality merchandise and found the arrangement very difficult to police. Private Portuguese trade flourished and local Asian trade patterns continued.

Trade was based largely on barter. For example, on Banda, the group of Moluccan islands where nutmeg trees grew, the inhabitants were accustomed to exchanging their spices for food and clothing, neither of which they produced themselves. They maintained the relative values of mace and nutmeg by selling mace seven times more expensively than nutmeg (the approximate ratio of production).

The Portuguese shipped spices to Lisbon, but for the first 60-odd years of the 16th century it was the Dutch who controlled shipping and trade in northern Europe, making handsome profits in their turn from the sale of spices. Then in 1568 Philip II of Spain moved into the Netherlands and war broke out. After 15 years the Dutch managed to dislodge the Spaniards from the northern, Calvinist provinces, but not from the Catholic south.

Genoa and Venice During the Middle Ages these rival city states became extremely wealthy and powerful. Eventually Venice won control of trade with the Orient.

Nutmeg and mace Introduced to Europe by the Crusaders, these prized spices did not become readily available until the sea routes to the Spice Islands were discovered.

Although the defeat of the armada in 1588 reduced Spain's sea power, Philip II was still able to deny the Dutch access to Lisbon for trade. They started to sail down the African coast and with information gathered from "spies" in Lisbon and from Jan van Linschoten, who returned after nine years in Goa with information about the spices, trading methods and Portuguese fortifications in the region, they planned their first voyage to Asia.

The rise of the Dutch East India Company

A group of Amsterdam merchants financed an expedition to the Indies in 1595. In many ways it was a catastrophic voyage; after two and a half years 89 men returned from a company of 248, brawling and arguing, but the

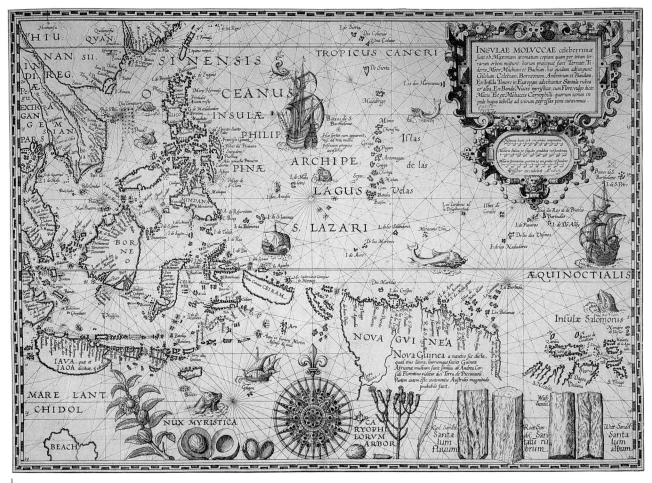

The Moluccas Also known as the Spice Islands, these were the main source of cloves, nutmeg and mace and the subject of much fighting between the Portuguese, the Dutch and the English in the 16th and 17th centuries.

merchants among them did have 245 bags of pepper, 45 tons of nutmeg and 30 bales of mace. This started a rush eastwards, with competing groups of merchants sending out expeditions. In 1602 the *Vereenigde Oost-Indische Compagnie* (United East India Company) was formed to put a stop to internal competition. Given sweeping powers, including the right to carry on the war with Spain in the Indies (at the company's expense), the VOC was the unwitting beginning of the Dutch colonial empire and also gave the Dutch the monopoly of the spice trade.

Portuguese superiority over the Asians was based on their naval and military strength; the Dutch soon proved themselves superior to the Portuguese in these fields as well. Their concerns were war and a monopoly on trade. Native rulers enlisted the help of the Dutch to rid them of the Portuguese, little realizing the consequences. In the first half of the 17th century the Dutch dislodged the Portuguese from Ceylon, the Moluccas and Banda, blockaded Malacca and established their main base at Batavia (Djakarta) on the island of Java. They tried to make contracts with native princes to buy at prices fixed by the company, paying in silver reals (Spanish coins) rather than allowing the barter system to continue, and obliging the natives to buy poor quality food and cloth at inflated prices from the company warehouses. They tried to stop all other trade, even by acts of piracy, to prevent Chinese and other traders selling spices to the Portuguese or the English. To control production the Dutch had nutmeg and clove trees uprooted and permitted plantings only on certain islands; native resistance met with near extermination and replacement by Dutch colonists, yet the output of spices increased. In 1622 the clove crop of Amboina and Ceram was twice world consumption, and even the colonists in Banda had to be asked to grow food crops instead of nutmegs because production was too great. To maintain prices in Europe huge quantities of spices were burned in the streets of Amsterdam.

The cost of this pursuit of monopoly was so immense that it is questionable whether the spice trade was profitable. By the 18th century spices were definitely on the deficit side of the company ledger. The man who masterminded the growth of the VOC was Jan Coen, a young book-keeper who sailed to the Indies in 1607, rose to become director-general of the VOC, then governor-general of the Indies, all within ten years. Virtually single-handed he created the Dutch empire, whose wealth was built on cloves, mace, nutmeg and Sumatran pepper.

English intervention in the spice trade

While the Dutch were displacing the Portuguese in the East, the English were also thinking seriously about trading voyages rather than piracy. In 1600 Elizabeth I granted a charter to an English company, but each expedition had to be financed separately, so that by 1609 the English had managed only to fit out 14 ships for five voyages - the Dutch usually sent a fleet of about this size every two years. In 1609 James I granted a new charter which gave the East India Company the monopoly of English trade with the East. A period of constant harassment between the Dutch and the English followed. In 1619 the new Dutch Republic signed a treaty with England which said that they should join forces and divide the spoils of the Indies, especially the Moluccas. For helping to fight the Spaniards and Portuguese, the English were to get one third of the Moluccan trade. The English were not strong enough to sustain the agreement; Coen sabotaged it and the English moved out of the Spice Islands to Macassar. They still managed to trade, though, sending back cloves regularly over the next 60 years in spite of punitive Dutch expeditions in the Spice Islands. However, by 1682 the English had been driven back west of the Indonesian archipelago.

The Dutch monopoly was not to last for ever; about 1770 Pierre Poivre, a botanist who was administrator of the Ile de France (Mauritius), smuggled clove and nutmeg trees out of the Spice Islands and cultivated them successfully. New plantings were made in other French tropical colonies - the Seychelles, Réunion and Cayenne, and later in Zanzibar and the West Indies. In 1795 the English planted clove trees on Penang. By the 19th century no European country had a monopoly on any spice and prices started to fall.

A caravel The fastest and most sea-worthy vessels in the 15th and 16th centuries, caravels played a significant role in the discovery of new routes to the East and West.

Spices from the West

Six years before Vasco da Gama reached the East, Columbus made landfall on the Caribbean island of Hispaniola and subsequently on the mainland of America. He made four voyages westwards, still looking for the fabled riches of China; instead he brought back tobacco, yams, kidney beans, many new fruits and nuts, and the chilli pepper. Some years later the allspice berry, recorded on the second voyage, became popular in Europe. In 1519 Hernan Cortés led his troops on the conquest of Mexico, eventually bringing back to Spain not only great wealth in gold and silver but also vanilla, chocolate, turkey, maize, tomatoes and potatoes. The Spaniards planted ginger in their New World colonies, capsicums in the Mediterranean region and in the East.

Trading in the Moluccas This was based largely on barter.

American entry into the spice trade

The United States entered the spice trade towards the end of the 18th century. Ships from Salem, New London, New Bedford, and Boston sailed for the East carrying tobacco, foodstuffs and even ice to trade for tea, coffee, textiles and spices - particularly pepper, ginger, cloves, cassia and cinnamon. Pepper from Sumatra and from Malabar was by far the most important import, in quantity and in value.

The decline of the New England ports in the 19th century gave New York the lead in importing spices, a position it still holds, with almost 60 percent by value of US spice imports in 1988. Baltimore and San Francisco come second and third with 11 and 6 percent respectively.

Drying chillies *Trays of chillies drying in the sun in rural China.*

The spice trade today

The United States is now the largest importer of spices in the world, followed by West Germany, Japan and France. Singapore is the largest entrepot for spices, notably pepper, vanilla, cinnamon, cloves, anise, coriander and cumin. Hong Kong is a significant entrepot too, especially for ginger, chillies and cassia from China.

In 1986 the international trade in spices was estimated at 350,000 to 370,000 tons in volume and valued at more than US $1,000 million annually. Japan, West Germany and Saudi Arabia are growth areas; the American market is declining somewhat, with imports of black pepper, mustard and sesame - the three largest items - down quite substantially from 1987 to 1988, partly because smaller crops have resulted in higher prices. However, US imports of spice oleoresins (aromatic extracts) continue to rise.

Pepper is the most important spice imported in most markets, in terms of both volume and value. Next in importance are the capsicum spices - paprika, chilli and cayenne pepper. Cardamom accounts for a large share of the spice imports in the Middle East and North Africa (where it is used to flavour coffee) and in Sweden and Finland (where it is used in baking). Indonesia produces large quantities of cloves but also uses substantial amounts for its kretek cigarette industry. However, it is now almost self-sufficient, which has led to a significant drop in prices and severe export problems for Madagascar and Tanzania as stocks of unsold cloves rise. Cassia, cinnamon, nutmeg and mace figure prominently in the imports of West European countries and the United States; Mexico and Brazil also buy

Vanilla *As it is one of the three most expensive spices, a large proportion of vanilla flavouring on the market is synthetic - as much as 90 percent in the United States.*

substantial amounts of cassia; allspice is bought in large quantities by the USSR and the countries of eastern Europe. Ginger and turmeric sell in significant volume worldwide, as do aromatic seeds like coriander, anise, caraway and cumin - but the value of the seeds is low. Demand for anise, star anise and juniper comes mostly from distilleries for the production of anise-flavoured drinks and gin. Saffron, cardamom and vanilla remain the three most expensive spices; consumer demand for "natural" flavourings has given a small boost to the vanilla market, but synthetic vanillin still accounts for a very large percentage of vanilla flavouring.

Ninety percent of the international trade in spices is in whole spices; paprika is the only spice sold ground in significant amounts, and curry powder the only blend that has any commercial importance internationally. The producing countries invariably ship in bulk and spices are packed for the retail market by the importers. The remainder of the trade is made up of essential oils and oleoresins. The latter are finding a growing market with industrial food manufacturers who prefer them to natural spices because of ease of handling and storage, freedom from bacteria and consistency in quality. Oleoresins are highly concentrated and have to be diluted in alcohol or another solvent, or blended with a dry ingredient before they can be incorporated in a food product. India, Sri Lanka and Indonesia have flourishing oleoresin-producing plants, as do most industrialized countries.

Cloves *Indonesia produces large quantities of cloves and is now almost self-sufficient in supplies for its kretek cigarette industry.*

Exporting countries

India leads the export league in spices (principally pepper, cardamom, chillies, ginger, turmeric, cumin and other seeds, curry powder) followed by Indonesia (pepper, nutmeg and mace, cassia, ginger, cardamom, vanilla), Brazil (pepper, cloves, ginger), the Malagasy Republic - Madagascar (vanilla, cloves) and Malaysia (pepper, ginger). More than 80 percent of spice exports are from developing countries, and production and export are an important element of the agricultural economy; the incomes of thousands of peasant farmers are supplemented by growing spices as a secondary cash crop. Yet even an export value of more than US $1,000 million annually represents only half a percent of the value of exports of all agricultural and fishery products, and is much lower than the value of exports of staple crops such as sugar or coffee. Nevertheless spice exports make a healthy contribution to foreign exchange earnings.

In an effort to reduce fluctuations in earnings from spices the producer countries are trying to set up more efficient trading operations and marketing programmes, to match supply to demand more carefully, and to increase the value of their crops by trying to meet the health regulations and quality controls of importing countries more adequately. The International Pepper Community has existed for many years and successfully pooled information on disease control, processing, marketing and price stabilization, but other individual spices have not benefited from such international support. Now the International Spice Group, set up in 1983 with members from importing and exporting countries, aims to provide the forum where the concerns of both buyers and sellers can be considered.

Spice stall in Morocco *A colourful display of assorted spices including paprika, peppercorns, cumin and cinnamon.*

2

Spice index

A comprehensive photographic index of both common and lesser-known spices from ginger and cinnamon to screwpine leaves and grains of paradise, arranged alphabetically by botanical name. Each entry covers the origins and history of the spice, its cultivation, distribution, and culinary and traditional uses throughout the world. The index shows the different forms in which the spices are available – fresh, dried, whole, ground – evaluating their relative merits. It describes the aroma and taste of each spice and gives helpful suggestions for using spices to flavour foods.

Grains of paradise

The plant has pink or yellow showy, trumpet-shaped flowers.

T HE MOST INTERESTING OF the spices related to cardamom, now fallen into obscurity, grains of paradise have a hot peppery taste and replaced true pepper when its price was high. Indigenous to the coast of West Africa along the Gulf of Guinea, from Sierra Leone to the Congo, grains of paradise are also known as Guinea pepper or Guinea grains, and Melegueta pepper. In the 14th and 15th centuries, production of the spice was so important that the coast became known as the Grain or Melegueta Coast. From here it was taken across the Sahara and shipped to Europe from Tripoli; later Portuguese traders took it to Europe directly from the African coast.

Today, grains of paradise feature almost exclusively in West African cookery. They are not easy to obtain but can occasionally be bought from suppliers of herbal medicines. A mixture of pepper and a little ginger has been used as a substitute.

Seeds These are a red-brown, chestnut colour and have the form of a tiny blunt pyramid. Between 60 and 100 seeds are enclosed in the red-brown fruit of the plant.

Ground The seeds are white inside and grind down to a fine aromatic powder.

Tunisian five spices Grains of paradise are one of the ingredients in this North African spice blend (p.109).

Mulled wine spice mix In the past, grains of paradise were popular ingredients in spice blends for mulling wine.

CULTIVATION
Distribution Cultivated in Ghana, Guinea, the Ivory Coast and Sierra Leone; most exports today are from Ghana.

Appearance & growth Grains of paradise are the seeds of a perennial reed-like plant that grows to a height of 2m (6ft).

Harvesting The seeds are removed from the bitter white pulp of the ripe fruit and allowed to dry before use.

Aroma & taste The grains taste pungently hot and peppery, without the camphor element that some cardamoms have; their odour is similar but fainter.

USES
Culinary In the past, grains of paradise were used to spice wine and beer. A popular tonic in the 17th century, especially in hot sack, today grains of paradise are little used in Western cooking. They are a valued seasoning in West Africa and

to the north in the Magreb, where they are one of the components of ras el hanout (pp.96-7). Grains of paradise are excellent in mulled wine, in braised lamb dishes, and with potatoes and aubergines.

Medicinal Used in West African herbal remedies, grains of paradise relieve flatulence and also have stimulant and diuretic effects. The seeds are an ingredient in a number of veterinary medicines.

Dill

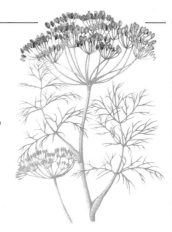

T HE NAME DILL comes from old Norse *dilla* meaning "to lull". Dill water was believed to have a soothing effect on the digestive system and was given to babies to relieve hiccups and colic. Grown for both its seeds and its leaves, dill has been known since antiquity. In medieval times, it was considered a magic herb to be used against witchcraft, and as an ingredient in love potions, while it was popular in the kitchen as a condiment. It was cultivated in England from the 16th century but was not introduced into the United States on a commercial scale until the 19th century. It is now grown in a number of countries, mostly in the northern hemisphere.

Anethum sowa, Indian dill, resembles the European plant, but the seeds are longer and narrower, the ridges are paler, and they taste slightly different.

The plant has thin, feathery leaves and clusters of tiny seeds.

Whole *Mid-brown with a lighter tan rim, the seeds are curved, oval, and flattish, with five ribs, two of which form a broader rim. The seeds are extremely light; 10,000 seeds weigh about 25g (1oz).*

Dill weed *The leaves are aromatic, adding a hint of anise to salads, vinegars, pickles and fish dishes.*

Seed head *The aromatic, tiny yellow flowers turn to seeds in late summer.*

Ground *Crush whole seeds as required.*

Essential oil *Used in commercial food flavourings.*

CULTIVATION

Distribution Native to southern Russia and the Mediterranean region; the main producers of dill today are Poland, Russia, Scandinavia, Turkey and the UK.

Appearance & growth Dill is a hardy annual that grows up to 1m (3ft) tall and produces clusters of small yellow flowers in the summer. It likes a sandy soil and good sunlight.

Harvesting To obtain good dill weed, the plant is cut before flowering. For seeds, the fruits are left to mature on the plant. Harvesting of the fruits begins when they turn yellow-brown, and is usually carried out when the dew is on the plants. The seeds are threshed, then dried.

Aroma & taste The aroma faintly resembles that of caraway, but is not as pronounced. Its taste is warm, pungent and slightly sharp. It lingers in the mouth for some time if the seeds are chewed on their own - quite a good way of eliminating less agreeable tastes.

USES

Culinary Pickled cucumbers, or dill pickles, have been favourites on both sides of the Atlantic for many years. In Scandinavia, both the leaves and seeds are much used in breads, with potatoes and with seafood. In Poland and Russia, dill is added to soups and stews, and the French use the seeds in cakes and pastries.

Medicinal In addition to its use in the relief of digestive problems, dill has been taken by nursing mothers to stimulate milk.

Celery

In summer, clusters of pale yellow flowers are succeeded by green seeds.

THE CELERY PLANT known to us today was developed from wild celery, or smallage, a common European plant found on marshy ground, especially near the sea. Smallage was used in ancient times as a medicine. To our palates it would have a very bitter taste, but it was popular with the Romans as a flavouring. To them it also signified ill-fortune and death, and smallage leaves were used to make wreaths.

In the 17th century, Italian gardeners bred out the bitterness of smallage and today, garden celery is grown for its stalks, leaves, seeds, essential oil, and in the case of one variety, celeriac, for its root. Celery seeds enhance or introduce a celery flavour to dishes but are not always easy to obtain. Celery salt is more available, but it soon develops a stale taste.

Seeds The tiny seeds are 1-1.5mm long and very light - approximately 75,000 seeds weigh 50g (2oz). They are mid- to dark brown, with five lighter ridges. Stalk ends are sometimes still attached.

Ground Good in drinks such as Bloody Mary, but for most purposes the tiny seeds can be used.

Celery salt A salt-based seasoning flavoured with the essential oil.

Essential oil Provides a savoury flavour.

Leaves These can also be bought dried and are used to flavour soups and casseroles.

Celery stalks Eaten on their own, with salad, or braised as a vegetable.

CULTIVATION

Distribution Native to southern Europe, celery is grown today from Scandinavia to North Africa, in North America and northern India.

Appearance & growth Celery is a member of the parsley family that grows to 1.2m (4ft). It thrives in a moist, cool climate in sandy loam. It has branched, fleshy, ridged leaf stalks, and dark green leaves.

Harvesting In its first year of growth, celery is harvested as a vegetable. From the second year, the seed heads are dried and the seeds are beaten from them.

Aroma & taste The seeds have a pronounced, celery-like smell. They taste warm and rather bitter, with a hint of nutmeg and parsley.

USES

Culinary Celery seeds are used in the food industry: in pickles, tomato ketchup, and tomato juice. In domestic cooking they are not as widely used as they might be. The Scandinavians and Russians add them to sauces and soups, and the seeds give a pleasant warmth to dressings for winter vegetable salads. Try the seeds with fish, in egg dishes, in stews, and sprinkled over bread.

Medicinal Until the 19th century, the essential oil was recommended as a cure for rheumatism. Celery is believed to be a tonic for asthma and herbalists use it to treat liver diseases, bronchitis, fever and flatulence. Celery seed tea is said to promote rest and sleep.

Mustard

KNOWN FOR THOUSANDS of years, mustard has always had manifold uses. Its English name comes from the Latin *mustum ardens* "burning must" because the ground seeds were mixed with grape must (unfermented grape juice). In the first century AD the Roman writer Pliny noted that mustard "has so pungent a flavour that it burns like fire". He also listed 40 remedies based on mustard.

In medieval Europe, mustard was the one spice ordinary people could afford to flavour their bland, monotonous diet. At the end of the 15th century, the Portuguese navigator, Vasco da Gama, took mustard on his voyage to the East; when the exotic spices he returned with became more widely accessible in Europe, mustard declined in popularity.

Mustard plants bear smooth or hairy seed pods, depending on the variety.

White mustard *The pale, sandy-brown or yellow seeds of the white form are larger than black, brown or Oriental seeds. They are much less pungent, but have excellent preservative qualities.*

Oriental seeds *A form of Brassica juncea, used by the Japanese in cooking and as a condiment.*

Brown mustard *In large-scale farming, brown mustard has replaced black. Black and brown seeds look very similar, but brown seeds are less pungent. The names black and brown are often interchanged.*

Black mustard *Now grown only in peasant economies.*

Crushed *Yellow seeds, which have been ground just enough to crack them.*

Powder *Finely ground mustard seeds are used in many smooth blended mustards.*

Essential oil *This is highly caustic.*

CULTIVATION

Distribution Black mustard is native to southern Europe and temperate western Asia. Brown mustard is native to India. White mustard has long been naturalized in much of Europe and North America. It is grown in most temperate countries.

Appearance & growth All the mustards are annuals and produce small yellow flowers. White mustard is hardy, grows to about 80cm (2¹/₂ft) and flourishes in heavy sandy loam. Black mustard is taller and grows best in rich soil. Brown mustard is closely related but is smaller with paler flowers.

Harvesting Mustard pods must be harvested before they burst, but when fully ripe. They are stacked in sheaves to dry, then threshed.

Aroma & taste If you chew a brown mustard seed, the taste is slightly bitter, then hot and aromatic; white mustard seeds have an initial sickly sweetness, followed by mild heat; black seeds have a strong, pungent flavour. Unlike other spices, the seeds have virtually no smell.

USES

Culinary White seeds are used as a pickling spice. Brown seeds are an important flavouring in southern India. Before they are added to a dish, they are usually heated in hot oil to bring out their nutty flavour.

Medicinal Less widely used today than in the past, mustard induces vomiting, and is considered a diuretic and stimulant. In traditional medicine, mustard plasters are a common treatment for arthritis and rheumatism. **Caution:** mustard plasters can irritate sensitive skins.

Blended mustards

THERE ARE TWO basic types of prepared mustard: those that are smooth and those that contain whole seeds. They may be flavoured with herbs, chillies, peppercorns, citrus fruits, soft berry fruits, champagne or sherry. They can be mild or fiery, lightly aromatic or pungent and eye-watering.
Initially mustard was prepared at home; the seeds were pounded in a mortar and mixed with vinegar, and sometimes with honey and other spices. Then sauce and vinegar makers started to prepare mustards. By the 14th century Dijon was firmly established as a mustard-producing centre, well supported by the gourmand Dukes of Burgundy.

Bordeaux mustard
The other principal type made in France. It has a darker colour, a hint of sweetness and is often flavoured with herbs such as tarragon. It has a mild, less well-defined taste than Dijon.

English mustard *Made by mixing mustard powder with water, and leaving it to stand for ten minutes so the flavour develops.*

Dijon mustard *Legally, this can be made anywhere in the world; the name refers to a style of mustard that is pale, smooth and clean tasting, made with brown mustard seeds, water, white wine, salt and spices. The city remains the mustard capital of France, producing about 80 percent of the country's output. Since 1937 Dijon mustard has been an appellation contrôlée.*

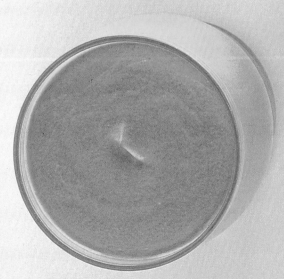

American mustard *The essential accompaniment to the hot dog and hamburger, American mustard is bright yellow and has a mild, clean taste. It is usually made from white mustard. Americans are also fond of sweet mustards that go well with ham.*

German mustard
This is sweetish, often flavoured with herbs and spices, and well suited to German sausages. Düsseldorf is the main mustard town of Germany.

Small mustard workshops were established, where black or brown seeds were crushed between huge, round stones, and then mixed with grape juice to make a paste. In the 17th century, a French mustard-maker, Bornibus, discovered a method of pressing mustard into tablets; these were manufactured in Dijon.

In the 1720s, a process of grinding mustard to a fine dry powder was developed. This caught on because it could be kept indefinitely. Early in the 19th century Jeremiah Colman started producing a high-quality mustard flour, which is still popular in England today.

Champsac mustard
An aromatic dark brown smooth mustard, flavoured with fennel seeds.

Herb mustard *This smooth, mild French mustard is lightly flavoured with mixed herbs.*

Beaujolais mustard
A fruity bilberry-coloured blend of coarse-ground mustard seeds and red wine.

Champagne mustard *A smooth, pale mustard, blended with champagne. Its mild flavour complements spicy foods.*

Red mustard *Made from whole mustard seeds and chillies, this pungent mustard goes well with bland foods.*

Wholegrain mustard
Whole mustard seeds give a crunchy texture to this hot English mustard.

Honey mustard
Made from coarse-ground mustard seeds, honey, raw sugar, vinegar and spices, this mustard has a sweet flavour.

Chillies

C. frutescens

C. annuum

MEMBERS OF THE capsicum family, chillies and sweet peppers come in all shapes, sizes and colours, ranging from tiny, pointed, explosively hot birdseye chillies, to large, fleshy peppers with a mild flavour. Indigenous to Central and South America and the West Indies, they had been cultivated there for thousands of years before the Spanish conquest, which eventually introduced them to the rest of the world. Columbus wrote that in the Caribbean island of Hispaniola *axi* (an Indian name for capsicum) was stronger than pepper and that people would not eat without it. On Columbus's second voyage in 1495, de Cuneo wrote: "In those islands there are also bushes like rose bushes, which make a fruit as long as cinnamon, full of small grains as biting as pepper; those Caribs and the Indians eat that fruit like we eat apples".

In 1569 the celebrated doctor Nicolas Monardes wrote at length about chillies and their successful adoption in Spain in his book on plants of the New World. Echoing him, the 17th-century herbalist John Parkinson noted that in Spain and Italy chillies were: "set in pots about the windowes of their houses". He also listed 20 types of capsicum, describing them as olive-shaped, heart-shaped, spear-like, cherry-shaped, and "broad and crumpled".

Today there are probably 200 different types of chillies grown in all parts of the tropics. They are used ripe, when they may be red, orange, yellow or purple, and unripe, when they are green. When buying fresh chillies, make sure they are crisp and unwrinkled. Ripe chillies are available dried, crushed, flaked and ground, and form the basis of many products (p.28). With pepper, ginger and turmeric, capsicums are the most widely cultivated spice crops today.

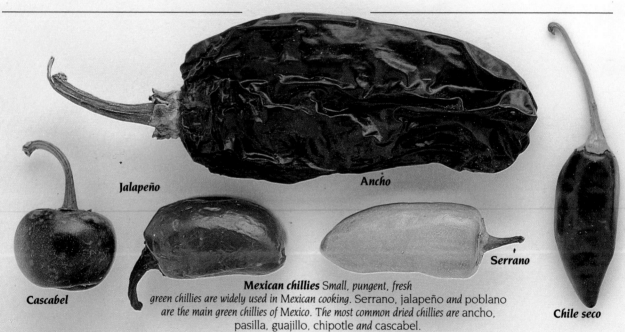

Jalapeño

Ancho

Cascabel

Serrano

Chile seco

Mexican chillies *Small, pungent, fresh green chillies are widely used in Mexican cooking. Serrano, jalapeño and poblano are the main green chillies of Mexico. The most common dried chillies are ancho, pasilla, guajillo, chipotle and cascabel.*

CULTIVATION

Distribution India has long been the largest producer of chillies and is a major exporter, along with Mexico, China, Japan, Indonesia and Thailand. All these countries are also great consumers of chillies. Sri Lanka, Malaysia and the United States are the main importers.

Appearance & growth Chillies are grown in the tropics from sea level to altitudes of 2,000m (6,600ft). Sweet peppers and chillies will grow in warm temperate zones too, but are susceptible to frost, and so are cultivated from seed in nurseries and transplanted later. C. *annuum* and C. *frutescens* are believed to come from one original species, so the two types are frequently confused. The C. *annuum* plant usually grows to 30cm-1m (1-3ft) high. Most sweet peppers, as well as some of the hot varieties, come into this group. C. *frutescens* is a perennial plant, which grows up to 2m (6ft); this species includes most of the small, pungent forms of chilli.

Harvesting Green chillies are picked three months after planting; other varieties, such as cayenne, are left longer to ripen. The harvest usually lasts three months. After picking, the chillies are either dried in the sun or artificially. Most chillies are grown annually as they become smaller and less pungent after the first year.

Aroma & taste Chillies have little aroma, but they vary in taste, from mild to fiery hot. Generally, the large, round, fleshy varieties are milder than the small, thin-skinned, pointed types. Capsaicin, the pungent principle that gives chillies their kick, is present in the seeds,

Guindilla

Morron

Spanish chillies *Mildly piquant and smoky dried chillies play an important part in Spanish cooking. Ñoras, romescos and choriceros have specific uses for flavouring foods such as salt cod a la vizcaina, romesco sauce and chorizo sausages.*

Ñora

Small chillies

Cayenne chilli *The long, thin cayenne chilli is quite widely available. It is very hot.*

Pickled chillies *These yellow-green pickled chillies are popular in Greece and Turkey as an appetizer.*

Fresh red and green chillies

Lombok *This pointed, rich red lombok is similar to the tabasco chilli. It is used in hot Indonesian dishes.*

Habanero chillies *From the West Indies, these lantern-shaped chillies in varying colours are bitingly hot.*

Birdseye chillies *Tiny, blistering-hot, pointed chillies, usually not more than 2cm (³/₄in) long.*

veins and skin in varying amounts, depending on the species and the state of ripeness. Try removing the seeds and the veins to reduce fire.

USES
Culinary In the tropics, chillies enhance the bland flavour of the staple foods: rice in India and Southeast Asia, beans and corn in Mexico, and cassava in South America. They provide the heat in curry powders, are used in pickling spice, in pepper sauces, chilli oils and essences. Chilli extracts are even used in ginger beer and other

drinks. **Caution:** When handling chillies, wash your hands well and avoid touching your eyes, and any sensitive areas or cuts (pp.154-5).

Medicinal Fresh capsicums are rich in vitamin C; they help in the digestion of starchy foods and may be taken as a tonic. **Caution:** In large doses, chillies may cause stomach and intestinal burns. Even when taken in small quantities, chillies can burn: soothe a sore mouth with plain rice, bread or beans. Do not drink: it will make the burning worse.

Chilli products

Cayenne
This very pungent, finely ground spice is made from a blend of small, ripe chillies of various origins.

Chilli flakes Made from dried, crushed chillies and used commercially in sausages, pickles, and sauces for pizza and pasta.

Paprika
A red powder, with a sweet or lightly pungent flavour and a faint bitter aftertaste. Essential for goulash, paprikash and many other Hungarian and Balkan dishes, it is also widely used in Spain.

Chilli powder The red powder is made from dried, ground chillies; the darker is an American invention, designed to flavour many southwest American and Mexican dishes. Ground chilli is mixed with other herbs and spices. Not all such mixtures are very pungent.

Red pepper A Turkish condiment, red pepper is prepared from moderately pungent capsicums of Turkey and southern America. The deeper the colour, the better the quality. When roasted to enhance the flavour, the colour darkens, as shown above right.

Chilli paste Often available in Oriental shops, this forms the basis of many fiery sauces.

Tabasco sauce This world-famous hot sauce is made from red chillies and vinegar.

Chilli oil Dried red chillies and vegetable oil have been heated together to make this pungent Chinese chilli oil.

Pepper sauce A golden, hot pepper sauce from the West Indies, where chilli sauces are served as a condiment with dishes.

Sambal In Indonesia, spicy hot pepper relishes, or sambals, are served in small dishes as an accompaniment to food.

Red-hot sauce Ginger adds a sweetish flavour to this biting chilli sauce from Malaysia.

Caraway

A MEMBER OF THE SAME aromatic family as parsley, caraway has been used since antiquity and cultivated in Europe since medieval times. The first-century epicure, Apicius, suggests flavouring vegetables with caraway, and describes a fish sauce containing caraway, oregano, mint, honey, oil, vinegar and wine. Medieval cooks added caraway to soups and to bean and cabbage dishes, and it was traditionally served with roast apples. Early recipes combine garlic, coriander and pepper with caraway. In the 17th century the herbalist John Parkinson notes in *Paradisi in sole* that "the seed is much used to be put among baked fruit, or into bread, cakes, &c to give them a rellish". He also tells us that seeds coated with sugar (comfits) were served with fruit as a digestive.

Caraway is frequently confused with cumin, particularly in Oriental cookery books, in which cumin is usually intended.

Caraway has feathery leaves and clusters of tiny whitish-green flowers.

Seeds About 4-7mm long, the curved seeds are tapered at the ends. The hard, brown seed shells have five lighter-coloured ridges.

Ground Although caraway is mostly used whole, it can be bought ground. It is easy to grind or pound your own at home.

Essential oil This has all the aromatic properties of the seeds, but in a more intense form. A few drops diluted in a teaspoon of water can help relieve flatulent indigestion.

Bread and cheese Rye breads and cheeses from countries such as Germany and Holland are often flavoured with whole caraway seeds.

CULTIVATION

Distribution Caraway is native to Asia and northern and central Europe. Holland is the world's major producer of the seed, followed by Germany, Poland, Morocco, parts of Scandinavia and the Soviet Union. It is also grown in the United States and Canada.

Appearance & growth A hardy biennial that grows to about 80cm (2¹/₂ft) high. Seeds appear throughout the summer. Caraway grows best in a rich light clay soil.

Harvesting The stems are cut once the fruit ripens. The seeds are then threshed and dried.

Aroma & taste Caraway has a pungent aroma which, like its flavour, is warm and slightly bitter. When combined with fruits and vegetables, caraway seems to add a hint of lemon.

USES

Culinary Popular in central European and Jewish cooking, caraway is used to flavour breads, sausages, sauerkraut, cabbage, soups and cheeses. In Alsace, local Munster cheese is traditionally served with a small dish of caraway seeds. Elsewhere in France, the seeds are also used to spice *pain d'épices*. The liqueur *kümmel* is flavoured with caraway.

Medicinal Said to relieve flatulent indigestion, colic and bronchitis.

Other uses The essential oil is used to flavour mouthwashes, gargles, perfumes and soap.

Cassia

O NE OF THE OLDEST of spices, cassia is native to Assam and northern Burma. It is recorded in a Chinese herbal in 2700 BC and in the Bible as one of the spices with which Moses was commanded to anoint the tabernacle (*Exodus* 30: 23-25). Arab and Phoenician traders took it to Europe in classical times.

The dried bark of a tree in the laurel family, cassia is sometimes known as Chinese cinnamon. Cassia and cinnamon, another member of the laurel family, are used interchangeably in many countries, and in the United States cassia is often sold simply as cinnamon. Although they are closely related, cassia is thicker and coarser and its taste is less delicate. In Britain, the two spices are differentiated. Cassia is used widely in America but is in less demand than cinnamon in Europe.

The tree has large shiny leaves and small, pale yellow flowers.

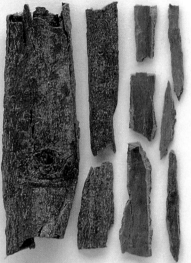

Ground *The bark is so hard it is usually ground commercially. The more pungent the smell, the better its quality.*

Essential oil *Popular as a flavouring in processed food, it is also sometimes used in inhalations to ease head colds.*

Bark *Available as flat, short pieces because it breaks easily. The outer layer of grey bark may be removed before cassia is dried. The inner bark is red-brown and easy to distinguish from that of cinnamon (opposite), which is finer and lighter in colour.*

Infusing cassia *When cassia or cassia buds are used as flavourings, they can be placed in an infuser for easier removal.*

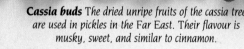
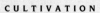

Cassia buds *The dried unripe fruits of the cassia tree are used in pickles in the Far East. Their flavour is musky, sweet, and similar to cinnamon.*

CULTIVATION

Distribution Cassia is grown in China, Vietnam, Indonesia and Central America, as well as Burma.

Appearance & growth A tropical evergreen that grows to about 3m (10ft) in height. The bark is rough and greyish-brown outside and smoother, reddish-brown within.

Harvesting This starts in the rainy season when the bark lifts easily. The bark is stripped from the tree, then dried on mats or wire netting. As it dries, it curls into quills which

are graded according to length, aroma and colour.

Aroma & taste Cassia has a more intense and less fragrant aroma than cinnamon. The taste is slightly sweet, with a bitter, astringent edge.

USES

Culinary Cassia seems better suited to savoury dishes rather than sweet. It is an essential spice in Chinese cuisine: ground, it is one of the constituents of five-spice powder (pp.72-3), but it is frequently added whole to flavour braised dishes and

spiced sauces. In India the spice can be found in curries and pilafs; in Germany and Russia, it is in demand to flavour chocolate. In many countries it is popular with stewed fruits, especially apple. Try it with grains such as couscous and pearl barley, and with split peas and lentils.

Medicinal Cassia is used as a tonic and a treatment for diarrhoea, nausea and flatulence.

Other uses Can be crushed and added to spicy pot-pourri blends.

Cinnamon

The tree has shiny leaves, yellowish-white flowers, and dark blue berries.

ONE OF THE FIRST spices sought in the explorations of the 15th and 16th centuries, true cinnamon is indigenous to Sri Lanka. Like cassia, it is the dried bark of a tree of the laurel family. There are references to it in the Bible and to its use in ancient Egypt, but it seems likely that cinnamon was confused with cassia, as it is not recorded in Sri Lanka until the 13th century.

The Portuguese occupied Sri Lanka for the spice until driven out by the Dutch in 1636. The Dutch began the cultivation of cinnamon, previously gathered in the wild, and kept prices high by burning excess supplies in Holland. Their monopoly of the trade ended in 1796 when the English East India Company took control. The trade became more competitive from the 1770s, however, when plants were taken to Java, India and the Seychelles.

Quills Cinnamon quills are assembled using the longest and best pieces of bark on the outside. They are rolled by hand to press the outside edges together, then rolled daily until properly dry, when they become tan in colour and are smooth, thin and brittle.

Quillings Broken quills are called quillings. Often these smaller pieces are rolled inside larger quills.

Ground It is possible to distinguish ground cinnamon from cassia by its tan colour, which is paler than the red-brown of cassia.

Essential oil Used widely in food processing and in the soft drinks industry. In aromatherapy, cinnamon oil is taken as an inhalation for colds and flu.

CULTIVATION

Distribution Native to Sri Lanka, also grown in India, Brazil, Indonesia, the West Indies, and Indian Ocean islands. The largest producer is Sri Lanka, followed by the Seychelles. Cinnamon from Sri Lanka is regarded as the best quality.

Appearance & growth The evergreen cinnamon tree grows to 10m (33ft) in the wild, but it is cropped to smaller, dense trees to ease harvesting. It thrives in a tropical maritime climate at a low altitude; and likes sandy soil.

Harvesting This is carried out in the rainy seasons: in Sri Lanka, between May and June, and October and November. The first harvest yields thick inferior bark. The quality improves with successive cropping and the finest bark comes from the thin shoots at the centre of the plant. Quills are assembled then dried in the shade as direct sunlight warps them.

Aroma & taste The agreeably sweet, woody aroma is quite delicate yet intense. The taste is well-defined, fragrant and warm.

USES

Culinary Suited to both sweet and savoury dishes, cinnamon is particularly good with lamb in Moroccan *tagines* and Iranian *khoraks*; in rice dishes; in fruit compotes (especially pear); in chocolate desserts, cakes and drinks; in spice breads; and as cinnamon toast. Cinnamon was once commonly used to flavour ale and wine, and it is still a good spice for mulled wine.

Other uses The spice is widely used in making incense, pomanders and pot-pourris (pp.148-51).

Coriander

The upper leaves are thin and feathery; the lower, broader and flat.

INDIGENOUS TO THE Mediterranean region, coriander is now cultivated worldwide. Its culinary and medical use has been documented for over 3,000 years: it is named in the Ebers papyrus of 1550 BC, in Sanskrit literature, and in the Bible: "Manna was like coriander seed, white" (*Exodus* 16:31). Hippocrates, the Greek "father of medicine", used coriander as a drug, and the Romans spread the use of the spice through Europe. It was one of the earliest spice plants to reach America and was grown in Massachusetts before 1670.

The fresh leaves of the plant are the ubiquitous green herb of southern Asia and South America, and the fruit is the spice, which has a completely different smell, taste and character. In most producing countries there is a large domestic demand for both herb and spice.

Whole (Moroccan) *More commonly available than the Indian variety, the seeds are spherical, ribbed, and 3-4mm in diameter.*

Ground (Moroccan) *Whole seeds are brittle and easy to grind to a fine powder at home.*

Leaf *A popular flavouring herb and garnish in Middle Eastern and Asian cuisines.*

Whole (Indian) *This has a sweeter flavour than Moroccan.*

Ground (Indian) *In India, coriander is usually dry roasted before grinding to enhance its flavour.*

Essential oil *Considered to be a digestive stimulant.*

CULTIVATION

Distribution Production is often small scale. India, Iran, the Middle East, the Soviet Union, the United States, and Central and South America all grow substantial crops.

Appearance & growth An annual, coriander grows from 30-80cm (1-2¹/₂ft) tall and bears small clusters of tiny white or pink flowers. The plant grows best in sunny situations.

Harvesting The seeds are picked when fully ripe; the plants are cut with the dew to avoid the seed pods

splitting, then dried, threshed and sieved. The spice is stored in sacks.

Aroma & taste The leaves and unripe fruits have a strong, fetid smell. The ripe fruits have a sweet, spicy-woody aroma with a peppery, balsamic note; their taste is mild, sweet, and slightly burning, with a clear hint of orange peel.

USES

Culinary Coriander is used in both savoury and sweet dishes. It is an essential ingredient in curry powder. In the Middle East, it is popular in

minced meat dishes, sausages and stews; in Europe and America it serves as a pickling spice and is used in baking. The classic French vegetable dishes *à la grecque* are flavoured with coriander. The essential oil flavours chocolate, as well as liqueurs and other drinks.

Medicinal The spice and the essential oil are used in pharmaceutical preparations for migraine and indigestion.

Other uses The essential oil is used in incense and perfumery.

Saffron

T HE MOST EXPENSIVE SPICE in the world, saffron costs ten times as much as vanilla, and 50 times as much as cardamom. The fact that the dried, thread-like stigmas of the saffron crocus are so light - over 20,000 produce only 125g (4oz) - and have to be hand-picked, accounts for their high cost.

Saffron was probably first cultivated in Asia Minor. It was used by all the ancient civilizations of the eastern Mediterranean, by the Egyptians and the Romans, in foods and wines, as a dye, in perfumes and as a drug.

By the seventh century, the plant was known in China, where it was in demand as a drug and a perfume. Three centuries later it was grown in Spain, probably taken there by the Arabs; in the 11th century it reached France and Germany; and England in the 14th century. Throughout this period, saffron was treated as a commodity of great commercial value, and severe penalties, even death, awaited anyone who adulterated it.

The blue-violet, lily-shaped flowers appear in autumn.

Threads *The stigmas are vibrant red-orange, or sometimes yellow, and wiry, about 2.5cm (1in) long. The deeper the colour, the better the quality. They are extremely light.*

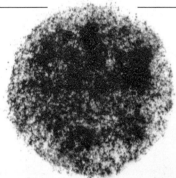

Ground *Mix ground saffron well with other ingredients to distribute its flavour evenly. It is preferable to buy threads, as ground saffron may be adulterated.*

**Carthamus tinctorius
SAFFLOWER**

Often known as bastard saffron, safflower is cultivated in China, India, the Middle East and Mexico. Unscrupulous merchants often try to sell it as saffron. Its colour is less vibrant and more regularly orange than that of saffron; the price is a fraction of saffron's cost. Safflower will colour food but not flavour it.

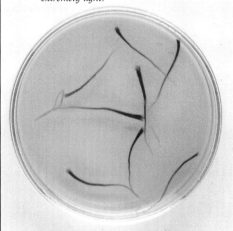

Infused *For even colouring, soak the stigmas briefly in a little hot water and add both saffron and water to the dish.*

Dye *For centuries saffron was used to colour cloth.*

Saffron bun
A mildly spiced traditional teacake (see also Saffron Bread, p.139).

CULTIVATION
Distribution Spain, Greece, France, Turkey, Iran, Morocco and Kashmir are the main producers. The best saffron is said to come from La Mancha in Spain.

Appearance & growth The saffron crocus is a perennial bulb that is planted in mid- to late summer. It grows to a height of 15cm (6in) and thrives in a sunny position in well-drained sandy soil.

Harvesting The flowers are picked once the petals open, which is usually in autumn. The stigmas are then hand-picked and dried.

Aroma & taste It has a distinctive, tenacious aroma and a penetrating, bitter, but highly aromatic, taste. A small amount will flavour a large dish and colour it a brilliant gold.

USES
Culinary Saffron is used less widely today than in the past, when it was added to sauces, soups and dishes for Lent. In Spain, it is a key ingredient in fish and rice dishes such as *zarzuela* and *paella*. It is used in France with fish, notably in *bouillabaisse*, and in Italy in *risotto*. It has long been used in England to make saffron cakes. Liqueurs, such as chartreuse, contain saffron.

Medicinal Prescribed in India for urinary and digestive problems. Research has revealed it to be rich in vitamin B2 and riboflavin.

Cumin

AN ESSENTIAL SPICE, cumin gives a distinctive warm flavour to an enormous range of savoury dishes in India, North Africa, the Middle East, Mexico and America. In the past it was used widely in baking, particularly in central and eastern Europe, but it is little used in European food today.

Cumin is often confused linguistically with caraway. In French, caraway was often referred to as *cumin des prés*, and inaccurate translations from Indian languages have confused *jeera*, which usually means cumin, with *shia jeera*, or caraway, which is little used in India. Black cumin (*kala jeera*) is a rare variety of cumin found in Kashmir, Pakistan and Iran. Sometimes called black caraway, it is used mostly in north Indian and Moghul cooking. It should not be confused with nigella (p.48), which has also been known by the same name.

Cumin's flowers are white or pale pink.

Seeds *Oval and 5-6mm long, with longitudinal ridges and a few little bristles. They are usually light brown, but may be greenish or greyish.*

Essential oil *Added to flowery scents of the violet, lily of the valley and hyacinth type.*

Black cumin *The seeds of this variety are smaller and have a sweeter smell.*

Ground *The combination of ground cumin and coriander leaves accounts for the characteristic smell of much Indian food.*

Curry powder *Cumin is one of the main constituents of curry powders (pp.80-1).*

Ground black cumin *The taste of black cumin falls between that of cumin and caraway; its smell resembles that of a haystack.*

CULTIVATION

Distribution Native to the Nile valley, but cultivation soon spread throughout North Africa and Asia Minor, and from there to Iran, India, Indonesia and China. From North Africa, cumin was taken to Spain and then to the Americas.

Appearance & growth An annual and a hot-climate plant, cumin grows to a height of about 30cm (1ft) and tends to sprawl.

Harvesting The stalks are cut when the seeds begin to turn yellow, then they are threshed and the seeds dried in the sun.

Aroma & taste The smell of cumin is quite pronounced: strong and heavy, with acrid or warm depths. Cumin seeds taste slightly bitter, sharp and warm, and their pungent flavour persists for some time.

USES

Culinary In India, cumin is generally dry roasted before use to bring out its flavour. Essential in mixtures such as garam masala (pp.84-5) and panch phoron (pp.82-3), it is also found in pickles, relishes and salads. In North Africa, it is an ingredient of ras el hanout (pp.96-7) and flavours *merguez* sausages and many couscous dishes. In the Arab countries further east and in Turkey, ground cumin is frequently added to minced meat dishes and to vegetables. In Spain it is combined with cinnamon and saffron in stews, and it is used in Texas in chilli con carne.

Medicinal Taken in India as a remedy for diarrhoea, flatulence and indigestion.

Turmeric

A MEMBER OF THE ginger family, turmeric is used throughout southern Asia for its musky flavour and attractive golden colour. On his travels in China, Marco Polo noted that turmeric was "a fruit that resembles saffron; though it is actually nothing of the sort, it is quite as good as saffron for practical purposes". He unwittingly set the tone for a major use of the spice in the West, where it frequently serves as a cheap substitute for saffron.

Turmeric is traded whole, and ground in the consuming country. It is available fresh in some Asian shops in the West.

Used for centuries in the East as a medicine and a dye, turmeric is also thought to have magical properties: on many islands in the Pacific, it is carried or worn as a protective charm to ward off evil spirits.

The plant bears large leaves and clusters of flowers in spikes.

Ground Mostly used and sold in this form. Turmeric's colour indicates its quality: the deeper the pigmentation, the better the spice.

Fresh The rhizome, or underground root, has a rough, segmented, light-brown skin. Inside it has bright orange flesh. It consists of a thick part and several stubby "fingers". These yield the best-quality turmeric.

Dried Turmeric is dried for export, during which time it loses about 75 percent of its original weight.

Turmeric dye A strong, golden-yellow.

CULTIVATION

Distribution India is the main producer. Turmeric is also cultivated in Indonesia, China, Bangladesh, South America and the Caribbean.

Appearance & growth A robust perennial that grows to a height of 1m (3ft), turmeric is usually propagated from "fingers", or small sections, of rhizome from the last year's growth. The rhizomes grow best in a hot, moist climate.

Harvesting The whole clump of the rhizome is lifted carefully to prevent any damage, and the fingers are broken off from the larger rhizomes. The turmeric is boiled or steamed, then dried. The outer skin is removed and the rough brown fingers become orange-yellow and waxy to the touch.

Aroma & taste Lightly aromatic, turmeric smells peppery and fresh with a hint of oranges and ginger. It tastes pungent, bitter and musky.

USES

Culinary Essential in curry powder, turmeric is also an important flavouring for many south Asian dishes. Indian vegetarian cooking relies heavily on it, especially in bean and lentil dishes, and in the West, turmeric is used commercially in sauces and in processed foods. It is often added to mustard blends.

Medicinal In Asia, turmeric is taken as a tonic and as a remedy for liver problems. Added to ointments, it is applied to treat skin diseases.

Other uses Turmeric is a traditional textile dye. In paste form, it is applied as a beauty mask in India.

Zedoary

A HIGHLY AROMATIC SPECIES related to turmeric, zedoary is native to India and Indonesia. During the sixth century it was brought to Europe by Arab traders and had some success in medicine and as a source of perfume, reaching the height of its popularity in the Middle Ages. In T'ang China, powdered zedoary or saffron and camphor were spread on paths where the emperor was about to walk.

The plant's large, fleshy yellow rhizome, or underground stem, is the source of the spice; it is sliced and dried, and used in Southeast Asian cooking. The rhizome also yields a light yellow essential oil. Medicinally, zedoary has similar properties to ginger, and it is used as a digestive aid in the East. Zedoary is almost unknown in the West; ginger can be used as a substitute.

The plant bears large leaves, red or green bracts and yellow flowers.

Ground Use as you would ground ginger, but remember that the taste of zedoary is somewhat bitter.

Slices
Greyish-brown in colour, the hard, dry slices of rhizome are about 2-4cm (³/₄-1¹/₂ in) in diameter. They have a rough, slightly hairy texture.

Perfume Zedoary is used in Indian perfumery.

Swedish bitters A herbal tonic, which contains zedoary extract.

CULTIVATION
Distribution Zedoary is grown throughout Southeast Asia in sub-tropical wet forest zones. It figures little in export trade.

Appearance & growth There are two kinds of zedoary, C. *zerumbet*, which is long, and C. *zedoaria*, which is round and stubby. The plant is propagated from small sections of rhizome, which are planted out in raked soil at the beginning of the monsoon. It grows to about 1m (3ft) high and takes two years to reach full development.

Harvesting Resembles that of turmeric (p.35). The rhizomes are then cut in slices and dried.

Aroma & taste The aroma is musky and agreeable, with a hint of camphor; it slightly resembles rosemary. The flavour is pungent and resembles that of ginger, but is not as bitter.

USES
Culinary In producing countries, zedoary is used as a spice in the preparation of condiments and in dishes in which turmeric or dried ginger might be used. It goes well with chicken and lamb in south Indian and Indonesian dishes. The young shoots of the plant are eaten in Indonesia, where the leaves are also used to flavour fish.

Medicinal A stimulant, zedoary is also rich in starch and is given to babies and invalids in India. It is combined with pepper, cinnamon and honey and used to treat colds.

Lemon grass

A TALL, TROPICAL GRASS with a bulbous base and a clear smell and taste of lemon, this handsome plant is found throughout Southeast Asia. The base and lower shoots of the plant are used in Southeast Asian cooking, and give a fresh, elusively aromatic taste to many Thai, Malay and Indonesian dishes. In the West, fresh lemon grass is available in some supermarkets, and Oriental shops keep the dried and powdered variety, as well as the fresh, often under the Indonesian name *sereh*. In Holland, look for lemon grass in Indonesian shops, where very fresh, long stalks are sold. It is fairly easy to grow as a houseplant: choose a stalk that has some bits of root, and put it in a pot of water; the roots will develop quite quickly. Once it is established, plant it in a large pot as it soon spreads.

Narrow, fibrous, pale green leaves grow from the bulbous base.

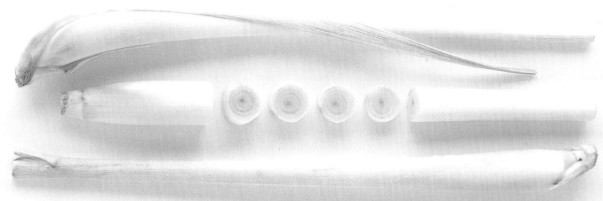

Fresh *The fleshy, fibrous stalk is slightly longer than a spring onion; cut it in small pieces and add directly to the dish.*

Dried strips *Dried lemon grass, processed into thin curly strips like lemon peel.*

Dried leaves *These are hard and fibrous and have little flavour.*

Powder *Add the powder straight to the dish; use sparingly.*

CULTIVATION

Distribution Native to tropical Asia; also cultivated in Africa, South America, Australia, Florida and California.

Appearance & growth A perennial tufted grass, lemon grass grows in dense clumps and thrives in a hot, sunny climate with some rainfall. It is better suited to sandy soil, which produces a higher content of the essential oil.

Harvesting The plants are harvested every three to four months.

Aroma & taste Distinctly lemon-like; lemon grass contains citral, also present in lemon peel, which is used in the production of artificial lemon flavours. Dried lemon grass doesn't have the clean, refreshing taste of the fresh variety. If you can't find lemon grass, use lemon balm or lemon peel as a substitute.

USES

Culinary A common ingredient in Southeast Asian cooking, lemon grass is often used whole or sliced in a clear soup, or is pounded to a paste with other ingredients and added to a stew. Lemon grass remains fibrous after cooking, so avoid chewing it. It combines well with garlic, shallots and chillies, and with fresh coriander to flavour fish, shellfish, chicken and pork.

Medicinal In the past, lemon grass was prescribed to relieve flatulence and as a sedative.

Other uses The essential oil, extracted by steam distillation, is used in perfumery.

Cardamom

The stems produce short flower stalks that bear small oval fruits after flowering.

CARDAMOM IS ONE of the most ancient spices in the world and one of the most highly valued: it is the third most expensive spice after saffron and vanilla. The seeds were prized in India long before the birth of Christ. Gradually, the spice reached Europe along the caravan routes and in ancient Greece and Rome it was an ingredient in perfumes, although it was valued too for its digestive properties and as a breath freshener. In India it is called the queen of spices, second only to pepper, the king, in economic importance.

Cardamom is also held in high regard in Bedouin culture. Tradition has it that before guests are served with cardamom coffee, the cardamom to be used is displayed. Its appearance is significant: plump, blemish-free pods imply esteem and respect for the guests.

Green cardamoms *Considered the best, these oval-shaped fruits are 5-10mm (¹/₄-¹/₂in) long. Each pod contains 12 to 20 dark brown or black highly aromatic seeds.*

White cardamoms *Thought to be more aesthetically appealing by some, these are simply bleached green cardamoms.*

Brown cardamoms *Not true cardamom, these pods are about 2.5cm (1in) long, and coarser in texture and flavour. They contain 40-50 hard, brown seeds.*

Seeds *Dark, often sticky, with a lemony, fresh flavour.*

Seeds *Black to light brown, with a sharp, breath-freshening taste.*

Seeds *Dark, sticky and hard, with a distinctly camphorous, almost antiseptic, taste.*

CULTIVATION

Distribution Cardamom grows wild in the rainforests of southern India and Sri Lanka at altitudes between 750 and 1,500m (2,500-5,000ft). It is now cultivated quite widely in Guatemala, Tanzania and Vietnam, as well as in its native habitat.

The green pods from Kerala, southern India, set the standards of quality and also price levels. International trade is in whole pods: whole green - fruits in which the colour has been preserved; whole bleached - bleached with sulphur dioxide when the colour has faded; whole straw colour - mature fruits dried in the sun; husked pods - usually when the capsule has split. India exports greens and a few bleached; Guatemala and Sri Lanka greens only. Tanzania exports sun-dried pods.

Appearance & growth A large perennial bush of the ginger family that grows to 2-5m (6-15ft) high.

Harvesting The first small harvest occurs three years after planting and

Related to true cardamom are plants of the Amomum and Aframomum genus. The seeds of many of these are marketed as cheap cardamom substitutes. Amomum subulatum, greater Indian or Nepal cardamom, is a native of the eastern Himalayas; a perennial plant growing up to 2m (6ft), with somewhat triangular-shaped fruits that are ribbed, and deep red when ripe, dark brown or black when dried. Amomum globosum, round Chinese cardamom, is also dark brown and rather hairy. It is often on sale in Chinese shops. Thailand trades in local Amomum species within Southeast Asia, which is also where most of the Javanese winged cardamom is used. Aframomum korarima from Ethiopia is another variety that is sold as a cheap substitute for green cardamom. The flavour of these other cardamoms is distinctly camphorous.

Ground cardamom Easy to adulterate, so it is better to grind your own powder as required.

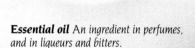

Essential oil An ingredient in perfumes, and in liqueurs and bitters.

Garam masala Essential in Indian cookery, cardamom is one of the main ingredients in this mixture (pp.84-5).

Cardamom-flavoured coffee A popular drink in Middle Eastern countries.

thereafter the plants bear for 10-15 years. The fruits ripen at intervals from September to December and are harvested every few weeks just before they ripen. If left to ripen on the plant they split open. After picking, the capsules are dried on open platforms in the sun, or on large plantations, in special drying rooms. The dried pods are hard, and the best are greenish in colour.

Aroma & taste The aroma of cardamom is mellow. Initially the taste has a penetrating note of camphor; it is sharply bitter and strong, and lingers quite long in the mouth if you chew a few seeds, but is warming and agreeable.

USES
Culinary Cardamom can enhance both sweet and savoury tastes. The pods themselves are inedible: all the flavour is held in the small, but very hard, seeds. In India, cardamom is one of the main components of garam masala and curry powders. It is also used in sweetmeats, pastries, puddings and ice creams. The Arabs put a few pods in the spouts of their coffee pots to give the drink a distinctive taste. In Europe, the Scandinavians are the biggest importers of cardamom for flavouring their spiced cakes, pastries and breads.

Medicinal Tincture of cardamom is considered a useful medicine for flatulence and stomach disorders. Chewing a few seeds cleanses the breath, particularly of excessive garlic. Together with betel leaves and areca nuts, cardamom forms part of the betel quid that Indians like to chew as a mouth freshener and digestive aid.

Cloves

ONE OF THE MOST important spices of commerce, cloves are the unopened flower buds of a small evergreen tree, native to the Moluccas, or Spice Islands, which today form part of Indonesia.

The earliest references to cloves are in ancient Chinese literature. Courtiers and officers of state were required to have a few cloves in their mouths when addressing the Emperor to keep their breath sweet. By the second century AD, cloves were part of the caravan trade to Alexandria, and their use slowly spread through Europe. By the 16th century, the Portuguese controlled the trade until driven from the Moluccas by the Dutch in 1605. They restricted the cultivation of clove trees to one island, and it was not until 1770 that the French smuggled seedlings to Mauritius and Bourbon. From there, plantations were eventually established on Zanzibar (now part of Tanzania) and in Madagascar, today's largest exporters.

Clove buds form in clusters at the ends of branches.

Clove infuser Used to add the flavour of cloves to foods without their texture.

Whole Look for cloves that are a bright, reddish-brown colour on the stem and lighter on the crown. They should be rough to the touch and snap cleanly. Good cloves will exude a small amount of oil if pressed with the fingernail.

Clove pomander An orange stuck with cloves is a traditional way to scent clothes (p.149).

Ground One of the ingredients of the Indian spice mix garam masala (pp.84-5).

Essential oil An antiseptic and analgesic, diluted oil of cloves can be used as a mouthwash or gargle. Rubbed on to the gums, it relieves toothache.

CULTIVATION

Distribution Indonesia produces the largest crop of cloves, followed by Madagascar (the Malagasy Republic), Tanzania, Sri Lanka, Malaysia and Grenada.

Appearance & growth Restricted to a height of 12-15m (40-50ft), clove trees take 20 years to reach full bearing, and then continue to bear fruit for about 50 years. They thrive in a tropical maritime environment.

Harvesting Harvested twice a year, from mid- to late summer and again in midwinter, cloves are picked when the buds reach full size but before the petals open. The buds are then dried over several days in the sun; they lose two-thirds of their weight and turn dark brown.

Aroma & taste Cloves have an assertive, dark aroma that is warm and rich. Tasted on its own, a clove is bitingly sharp, hot and bitter, and it leaves a lasting numb sensation in the mouth. Its effect is tempered by cooking and by other ingredients.

USES

Culinary Cloves go well with sweet or savoury foods and are used, for example, by Americans to stud a baked ham, and by the Germans in spiced breads.

Other uses Indonesian cigarettes are made with two parts tobacco to one part cloves. The essence is a food preservative.

Asafoetida

The whole plant emits asafoetida's distinctive smell.

A LITTLE-KNOWN SPICE outside India, asafoetida is a dried, resin-like substance obtained from the rhizomes of several species of *ferula*, or giant fennel. Its name derives from the Persian *aza*, resin, and the Latin *fetida*, which means stinking and describes this spice's most obvious attribute. Native to south-western Asia, asafoetida seems to have been much prized in Roman cooking. Called *silphium*, *laser* or *laserpitium*, it was imported from Persia and Armenia and the juice of both stem and root was used. It was a costly spice: the Roman epicure Apicius describes how to make an ounce piece last indefinitely by storing it in a jar with about 20 pine nuts. To flavour food, a few of the pine nuts were crushed and added to the dish. The nuts taken from the jar were then replaced.

Block Fresh asafoetida is pale in colour, some types darken eventually to a deep brown. A lump of asafoetida will keep its potency for several years.

To grind Break off small pieces and grind with an absorbent powder, such as rice flour.

Compound Often sold in Indian stores in this form, as granules or as a powder.

Granules Store asafoetida in an airtight container to prevent its smell from dominating.

Powder In Indian and Arab cuisines, a tiny amount enhances the flavour of dishes.

CULTIVATION

Distribution *Ferula* flourishes in the dry regions of Iran, Afghanistan, India and Pakistan.

Appearance & growth *Ferula* are smelly plants that grow to some 2-4m (6-12ft), depending on the species. They have soft-centred stems, finely toothed leaves, and produce clusters of yellow flowers.

Harvesting In spring, just before flowering, the stalks are cut to the root and a milky liquid exudes which dries to form asafoetida - a solid gum-like mass. The gum is scraped off and further cuts are made until the root dries up, which usually occurs after about three months.

Aroma & taste Powdered asafoetida has a strong, unpleasant smell, reminiscent of pickled garlic, which is caused by sulphur compounds in the volatile oil. The taste is bitter and acrid and decidedly nasty when sampled alone. However, when asafoetida is fried briefly in hot oil, the nastiness disappears and the oil takes on an onion taste.

USES

Culinary In western and southern India, asafoetida flavours pulses and vegetable dishes, pickles and sauces. A piece of asafoetida may be rubbed on a grill before cooking meat. It should always be used sparingly. In Iran, the centre of the stalks and the leaves are eaten as a vegetable.

Medicinal Asafoetida is said to have antispasmodic properties. It has been used in the past to treat hysteria and was sometimes taken as a sedative. In India it is prescribed to treat flatulence and bronchitis.

Fennel

THE ROMANS VALUED fennel's shoots as a vegetable and added the seeds to sauces for meats. The historian Pliny believed that strengthening eyesight was one of fennel's medicinal virtues, a belief endorsed by later herbalists.

Fennel has long been used in India and China, where the seeds were taken as a remedy for scorpion and snake bites, a use that spread to Europe. Our ancestors hung fennel over the door in the belief that it would guard them against witchcraft, and blocked the keyhole at night with ground fennel seeds to sleep undisturbed.

In 1418, when the Portuguese discovered Madeira, the fragrant smell of wild fennel led them to call the place where they landed Funchal, from *funcho*, the Portuguese word for fennel.

A graceful perennial with feathery leaves and small yellow flowers.

Seeds *Green to yellow-brown, the seeds are 5-10mm (^{1}/$_4$-^{1}/$_2$in) long, oblong, elliptical, straight or slightly curved, with prominent lighter ridges. They sometimes have a short piece of stalk attached.*

Essential oil *The seeds contain a high proportion of anethole, which is used in making pastis and other anise-based drinks.*

Ground *Grind the seeds to a fine powder as required.*

Seed head *Seeds form in clusters after the flowers have died away.*

CULTIVATION

Distribution Indigenous to the Mediterranean region but naturalized in many temperate countries, fennel is cultivated for export in Germany, Italy, France, Russia, the Middle East and India.

Appearance & growth The bright green stalks reach 1.5-2m (5-6ft) in height. The plant will grow in most conditions, although it prefers a sunny, sheltered spot.

Harvesting The seed heads are harvested just before the seeds ripen. To dry the seed heads, cover them with a paper bag and hang them indoors by the stems.

Aroma & taste The whole plant is aromatic and the seeds smell like anise. The taste is similar, too: warm and fragrant, but not as sweet, with a slight note of camphor.

USES

Culinary The Italians cook fennel with roast pork and add it to the excellent salami from Florence called *finocchiona*. In Iraq it is ground with nigella to flavour bread. The Indians use fennel seeds in vegetarian cooking, in breath-freshening *paans*, and candied to chew as a digestive aid at the end of a meal. In Europe, fennel is a traditional seasoning for fish, and it flavours pickles for cucumbers, sauerkraut and herring.

Medicinal An important medicinal plant in the past. The herbalist Culpeper noted that the seeds were used in medicines for shortness of breath and for wheezing. Fennel was also believed to help cure stomach complaints and toothache.

Star anise

ONE OF THE FEW spices used in Chinese cookery, star anise is native to southern China and Vietnam. A very pretty spice, it is the fruit of a small evergreen tree of the magnolia family. The shape of ripe star anise is that of an irregular, eight-pointed star. Its Chinese name means eight points.

The use of star anise has never spread much beyond its native region, although wherever the Chinese have settled, they have taken the spice with them. Old recipes reveal that star anise was used in the West in the 17th century, in fruit syrups and jams, and in recent years the spice has been rediscovered by Western chefs, and is often added to fish stews.

The tree bears shiny leaves and small, yellow, multi-petalled flowers.

Ground *The whole fruits are best ground in a mortar or electric grinder as required.*

Whole *When dried, star anise is hard and reddish brown. Each point of the star contains a glossy, brittle, brown seed.*

Seeds *These are less aromatic than the rest of the fruit.*

Chinese five-spice powder *The flavour of star anise dominates this mixture, which also contains fagara, cassia or cinnamon, cloves and fennel seeds (pp.72-3).*

Broken fruit *The fruit is generally used whole, or broken into pieces.*

CULTIVATION
Distribution Southern China and Vietnam.

Appearance & growth The tree grows to a height of about 8m (26ft) and bears small yellow flowers. The flowers are followed by fruits in the sixth year, and the tree continues to bear fruit for up to 100 years. As the fruit ripens, it opens out into a star shape with eight points, each of which is hollow and contains a seed.

Harvesting The fruits are picked before they ripen, then sun-dried.

Aroma & taste Although not related to anise and fennel, star anise has a similar smell and taste. It is more pungently liquorice-like and has a distinct sweet note.

USES
Culinary The Chinese often add star anise to poultry and pork dishes; it is also a key ingredient in five-spice powder. The Vietnamese use the spice in their beef soup, *pho*. It is an ideal flavouring for roast chicken, and goes well with braised fish, with scallops, and in clear soups. Try it with leeks and pumpkin.

The essential oil contains anethole, the principle aromatic constituent, also found in anise. It flavours liqueurs such as pastis and anisette, and is also used in chewing gum and confectionery.

Medicinal Star anise is used in the East to relieve colic and rheumatism and to flavour cough medicines. The spice is chewed whole to sweeten the breath.

Other uses The essential oil is used in soap making and in perfumery.

Juniper

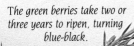

J UNIPER IS PROBABLY BEST KNOWN for the distinctive flavouring it gives to gin and other spirits and cordials. The berries come from a prickly evergreen shrub that grows throughout much of the northern hemisphere. Although one of the few temperate-climate spices that can be gathered in the wild or bought quite cheaply, juniper is largely ignored in the kitchens of English-speaking countries. The Scandinavians add juniper berries to marinades for pickled beef or elk, and to red wine marinades for roast pork. In northern France, the berries are used in venison dishes and pâtés; and, in Alsace and Germany, with sauerkraut.

Crushed berries can be mixed with salt and garlic and rubbed on to game birds before roasting. Combined with allspice and pepper, juniper is used for spicing beef.

The green berries take two or three years to ripen, turning blue-black.

Berries *These are about the size of a small pea. When freshly picked, they have a green-blue bloom which tends to disappear after drying. Berries grown in warmer latitudes have more flavour.*

Crushed berries *The purple-black, smooth berries are quite soft and easily crushed to show their brown pulp and seeds.*

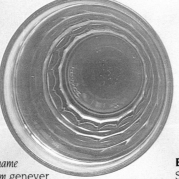

Plant *The shrub has sharp needle-like leaves, grouped in threes.*

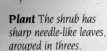

Gin *The name derives from genever, Dutch for juniper.*

Essential oil *Said to aid digestion and circulation.*

CULTIVATION

Distribution The plant grows wild throughout Europe and in America; most berries grown for commerce come from eastern Europe.

Appearance & growth Juniper is a coniferous shrub of the cypress family. After pollination, a pulpy covering forms round the seeds to produce berries, on female bushes.

Harvesting The ripe berries are gathered in the autumn and dried at a temperature below 35°C (95°F) to stop the essential oil evaporating.

Aroma & taste The pleasant aroma is bitter-sweet and unmistakably like gin. The berries taste sweet with a hint of pine and turpentine. They produce a slight burning sensation in the mouth.

USES

Culinary Juniper blends well with garlic; with aromatic herbs such as marjoram and rosemary; and with wine, beer, brandy and, especially, gin. Use it in marinades and sauces for pork and game; in brines and dry-salting mixtures; and in pâtés. Juniper marries well with veal and braised beef dishes and has a natural affinity with cabbage.

Medicinal Described by herbalists as a diuretic and an anti-inflammatory. **Caution:** Avoid juniper in pregnancy and if you have a kidney disorder.

Other uses The berries and roots yield purple and brown dyes. In the past, the leaves and berries were burned to purify the air, and the berries were applied to treat snakebites. The highly aromatic essential oil is added to some insecticides and perfumes.

Galangal

THERE ARE TWO MAIN TYPES of galangal: lesser and greater. Members of the ginger family, lesser galangal is native to southern China and greater to Indonesia. *Kaempferia galanga* (p. 64) is a similar rhizome, or underground stem, used medicinally in China. In Indonesia, lesser galangal is called *kencur* and greater galangal is known as *laos*. The latter is also known as *khaa* in Thailand and *lengkuas* in Malaysia, and may be sold under any of these names in Oriental shops.

Galangal was known in ancient Egypt where it was used as a fumigant. It reached Europe in the Middle Ages and was valued both as a medicine and a spice. Its use declined, however, and today galangal is rarely found outside Southeast Asia, except in Oriental communities. In England, the word *galingale* was formerly used for both galangal and the roots of the plant *Cyperus longus*.

Greater galangal has sword-like leaves and flowers with pink veins.

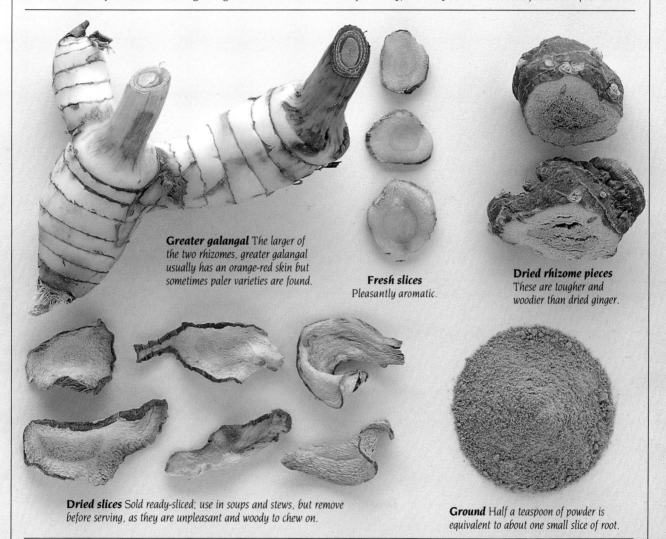

Greater galangal *The larger of the two rhizomes, greater galangal usually has an orange-red skin but sometimes paler varieties are found.*

Fresh slices *Pleasantly aromatic.*

Dried rhizome pieces *These are tougher and woodier than dried ginger.*

Dried slices *Sold ready-sliced; use in soups and stews, but remove before serving, as they are unpleasant and woody to chew on.*

Ground *Half a teaspoon of powder is equivalent to about one small slice of root.*

CULTIVATION

Distribution Both plants are today cultivated commercially in India and Southeast Asia.

Appearance & growth Lesser galangal reaches 1m (3ft) tall and has long, narrow leaves and small white, red-streaked flowers. Greater galangal, as its name suggests, is a larger plant that grows up to 2m (6ft). The rhizomes of both plants are knobbly and ginger-like.

Harvesting For both species, the rhizome is lifted, cleaned and processed in a similar way to ginger and turmeric.

Aroma & taste Lesser galangal has the more pungent aroma of the two galangals and has a hint of eucalyptus; its piquant taste is akin to cardamom and ginger. The flavour of greater galangal is like a mixture of ginger and pepper, with a sour, lemon-like note.

USES

Culinary Throughout Malaysia and Indonesia, both types of galangals are used fresh in curries and stews. Greater galangal is an essential component of Thai curry pastes (pp.78-9), and in Thai cooking is a much preferred spice to ginger. Lesser galangal is used in the manufacture of some bitters and liqueurs, and to flavour beers in Scandinavia and Russia.

Medicinal In Asian medicine, galangal is used to treat catarrh and respiratory problems. A drink made from grated galangal and lime juice is taken as a tonic in Southeast Asia. In the past, galangal was a treatment for flatulent indigestion.

Nutmeg & mace

M YRISTICA FRAGRANS is unique among spice plants as it produces two distinct spices: nutmeg and mace. It is a spreading evergreen tree, native to the Banda islands in the Moluccas, or Spice Islands. Nutmeg is the kernel of the seed; mace is the lacy growth, known as the aril, which surrounds the seed.

In the sixth century, nutmeg and mace formed part of the caravan trade to Alexandria. About the same time, nutmeg was being used in China as a medicine for digestive disorders. The Indians and Arabs valued the spice as a treatment for digestive, liver and skin complaints, and both nutmeg and mace were held to be aphrodisiacs.

The spices were probably brought to Europe by the Crusaders. They were used as fumigants and only became popular in the kitchen after the

The pale fruit resembles an apricot. It splits when ripe to reveal its seed.

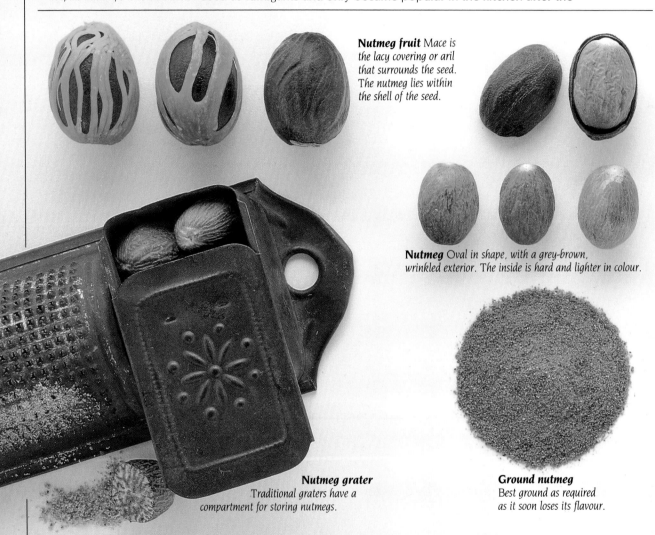

Nutmeg fruit *Mace is the lacy covering or aril that surrounds the seed. The nutmeg lies within the shell of the seed.*

Nutmeg *Oval in shape, with a grey-brown, wrinkled exterior. The inside is hard and lighter in colour.*

Nutmeg grater
Traditional graters have a compartment for storing nutmegs.

Ground nutmeg
Best ground as required as it soon loses its flavour.

CULTIVATION

Distribution Mace and nutmeg are native to the Moluccas, but are also cultivated in Sri Lanka, Malaysia, and the West Indies.

Appearance & growth The nutmeg tree is an evergreen that grows to 12m (40ft) or more in height. It has dark green oval leaves and small pale yellow flowers. Trees start to bear fruit in the seventh or eighth year, and continue to bear for up to 40 years. They are best suited to a tropical maritime climate, and thrive

in the rich volcanic soil of the Moluccas and the fertile loam of Grenada. Plantations are usually below 750m (2,500ft), and the trees are sheltered from high winds.

Harvesting The fruit ripens six to nine months after flowering, and is usually gathered when it falls to the ground. The outer husk is stripped off and the mace is removed, pressed flat and dried on mats. This process may take as little as two to four hours, during which time the mace retains its scarlet colour. Once the mace has been removed, the

seeds are dried on trays for four to six weeks until the nutmegs rattle in their outer shell. They are cracked open and the nutmegs removed, then graded according to size and quality. "Defectives", "shrivelled" and "bwp" (broken, wormy, punky) nutmegs are sorted out from the rest, which are graded by size as 80s or 100s, and so on, according to the number in the pound.

Aroma & taste Mace and nutmeg are similar in aroma and taste, but mace is more refined. The aroma is rich, fresh and warm. The taste is warm

Portuguese developed the trade in the Spice Islands in the 16th century. Nutmeg became important as both a medicine and a spice, and by the late 16th century, it seemed to be the cure for just about everything. By the 18th century, people carried their own nutmegs, together with small, ornamental graters of silver, wood or bone, to flavour food and drinks such as hot ale, mulled wine, or possets (curdled milk drinks).

Control of the nutmeg and mace trade passed from the Portuguese to the Dutch and eventually, towards the end of the 18th century, to the English. The English planted nutmeg trees in Penang, Sri Lanka and Sumatra, and in the following century, trees were taken to Grenada in the West Indies, where almost a third of the world's nutmeg is produced today.

Mace *The scarlet aril turns red-orange or orange-yellow by the time it reaches the market, depending on its source.*

Mace blades *Indonesian blades tend to be orange-red; those from Grenada are generally orange-yellow.*

Essential oil of nutmeg
Used in creams designed to relieve rheumatism.

Ground mace
When ground, mace keeps its flavour longer than some ground spices.

Coarse ground mace *The blades are hard to grind to a fine powder with a pestle and mortar - use a coffee grinder.*

and highly aromatic - sweetish in nutmeg and more bitter in mace.

USES
Culinary In Southeast Asia, China and India, both spices are used sparingly. In India they are found mostly in Moghul dishes. The Arabs have long added nutmeg to mutton and lamb, but the Europeans have used nutmeg and mace most extensively in both sweet and savoury dishes. Nutmeg is a standard seasoning in many Dutch recipes, and graters resembling pepper mills are a common

household item there. The Dutch add nutmeg to mashed potato, white cabbage, cauliflower and vegetable purées; to macaroni; to meat stews; and to fruit puddings. The Italians enjoy nutmeg with mixed vegetable dishes, and veal, and in fillings and sauces for pasta.

Nutmeg is widely used in honey cakes, rich fruit cake, fruit desserts, and fruit punch. It goes well in stews and meat pies, and in most egg and cheese dishes, as does mace.

Mace gives a lift to bechamel and onion sauce, clear soups, shellfish stock, potted meat, cheese soufflés

and cream-cheese desserts. In Indonesia, the flesh of the fruit is used to make a sweetmeat.

Medicinal More common in Oriental than in Western medicine, nutmeg is used to relieve bronchial disorders, rheumatism and flatulence. In large quantities it may cause drowsiness, hallucinations and euphoria, and an excess can be fatal.

Other uses Nutmeg is used in perfumery, soaps and shampoos.

Nigella

Nigella is the botanical name for the plant we know as "love-in-a-mist", which is cultivated in gardens for its delicate blue flowers and feathery foliage. The species of nigella grown for its small black seeds is a close relative, but less decorative in appearance. Until the 17th century, nigella was more popular in Europe. The herbalist Gerard describes the seeds as "... of a blackish colour, very like unto onion seed, in taste sharpe, and of an excellent sweet savour". They were used in sweet waters and powders, and ground seeds were wrapped in a piece of cloth and gently heated in the belief that they helped to restore the sense of smell.

The plant has ragged, grey-green leaves and delicate, five-petalled flowers.

In India, where nigella seeds are commonly used as a flavouring, there is much confusion about their name. In the north of the country, where nigella grows wild, they are called *kala jeera*, or black cumin. Real black cumin (p.34) is also known as *kala jeera* as well as *shahi jeera*, or royal cumin. In much of India, nigella seeds are known as *kalonji* (black onion seeds).

Seeds These are a deep, dull black, 2-3mm long and angular. They have five prominent spikes.

Ground Use a coffee grinder to grind the seeds to a powder.

Nan Bread baked in the clay tandoor ovens of northern India, nan is flavoured with nigella.

Panch phoron Nigella features in many Indian spice mixtures including panch phoron (pp.82-3), curry blends and masalas.

CULTIVATION

Distribution Native to western Asia, southern Europe and the Middle East, nigella is most widely cultivated in India.

Appearance & growth A hardy annual raised from seed, the plant grows to 60cm (2ft).

Harvesting The seed capsules are gathered as they ripen but before they burst. They are then dried and crushed so that the seeds can be removed easily.

Aroma & taste The aroma of nigella is not strong. The taste is nutty and acrid, like a cross between poppy seeds and pepper; it is reminiscent of oregano.

USES

Culinary In India, nigella is used whole to spice vegetables and pulses, usually after it has been dry roasted to heighten its aroma and flavour. It is an ingredient of several spice mixes and is sprinkled on breads. It is also used to season bread in the Middle East and in Turkey. Nigella is a spice to experiment with; it complements the spices coriander and allspice, and the herbs savory and thyme.

Other uses It is believed to be an insect repellant.

Poppy

THE OPIUM POPPY is a plant of great antiquity. Its botanical name translates as sleep-inducing poppy, and refers to the plant's narcotic properties, as opium, which oozes from the unripe seed pods if they are cut, contains compounds from which morphine and codeine are extracted. These are not present in the ripe seeds. The plant has been cultivated for opium and its seeds from earliest times. A Cretan statue of a poppy goddess of about 1400 BC shows the seed pods cut to extract the opium, just as they are today. A mix of roasted white poppy seeds and honey was popular with wealthier Romans.

By the time of Mohammed (AD 572-632) opium was known for its medicinal and narcotic properties in Arabia and Asia. It was used to relieve cholera, malaria and dysentery, but increasingly as a habit-forming drug in India and China. The great demand for opium made fortunes, legal and illegal.

As the flower dies back, it reveals a bulbous seed capsule.

Creamy-yellow seeds *Common in India, these kidney-shaped seeds are about 1mm long. A thousand seeds weigh only 0.5g.*

Brown seeds *In Turkey, these seeds are mixed with grape syrup and nuts to form a dessert.*

Blue-grey seeds *Slate-blue seeds are most common in Europe. Like the other varieties of seeds, they are hard and clean looking.*

Ground seeds *Crush the seeds in a pestle and mortar or grind in a coffee grinder. In India, white ground seeds act as a thickening agent in sauces.*

Paste *Roasted seeds are ground to a paste to form the basis of many Turkish dishes.*

Seed head
The brownish-green seed capsules vary greatly in shape and size, but all have a ribbed outer casing, crowned with a stigma. Inside, there are several chambers containing hundreds of tiny seeds.

CULTIVATION
Distribution Native from the eastern Mediterranean to central Asia; India, China, Iran, Turkey, France, Holland and Canada are the main producers.

Appearance & growth A tall annual raised from seed, the plant bears pale white to violet flowers.

Harvesting When the seed heads turn yellow-brown, the plants are usually harvested mechanically, then stacked like corn stooks, or the capsules are cut off and dried.

Aroma & taste Poppy seeds have a slight but pleasantly nutty aroma, and a similar but more pronounced taste, with an underlying sweet note. They have no narcotic properties.

USES
Culinary In Western and Middle Eastern cooking, poppy seeds are mainly sprinkled on breads and cakes, or crushed with honey or sugar to make pastry fillings. In Turkey they are made into halva or desserts; in India the seeds are usually ground with other spices and

used to thicken and flavour sauces for meat and fish. Try adding poppy seeds to dressings for noodles or rice, or to garnish vegetables. Roast first to strengthen their flavour.

Other uses The seeds are an important source of oil. The odourless oil from the first cold-pressing of the seeds has a light almond-like taste and is a good salad oil. Oil from later hot-pressings is used in soap and ointments and, after bleaching, in the manufacture of artists' paints.

Allspice

A TROPICAL SPICE, grown mainly in Jamaica, the reddish-brown allspice berry was introduced to Europe by Columbus and his fellow explorers, who found it growing in the Caribbean islands and mistakenly thought it was pepper, hence its Spanish name, *pimienta* (pepper). Later anglicized as pimento, allspice subsequently became known as Jamaica pepper.

When the English conquered Jamaica in 1655, they acquired an established trade based on substantial plantations; wild fruits were no longer part of its commerce. Jamaican exports increased more than 20·fold between 1755 and the end of the 19th century. Although colonists planted trees elsewhere in the tropics, they did not thrive, and allspice is the only important spice that still comes almost exclusively from the New World.

The berries turn from green when unripe, to purple-brown when ripe.

Whole *The red-brown berries are about the size of a small pea and have a somewhat rough surface. Most of the flavour is in the outer shell rather than in the seeds inside.*

Ground *It is preferable to buy allspice whole and grind it as needed.*

Essential oil *A common ingredient in men's spice-based perfumes.*

Pimento dram *A rum-based drink flavoured with allspice, similar to the Clove Cordial recipe (p.145).*

Pickling spice *Allspice is an essential ingredient in this traditional mixture used for pickling fruit and vegetables (pp.102-3).*

Spiced tea mix *Blend with tea and other spices for a warming drink (p.145).*

CULTIVATION

Distribution Native to the West Indies and Central and South America; the best allspice comes from Jamaica.

Appearance & growth An evergreen, the allspice tree grows to about 9m (29ft) in height. It has dark green, glossy leaves and clusters of small white flowers in the summer. The trees begin to bear fruit when six to seven years old and can continue to bear for up to 100 years. A ratio of ten female trees to one male is the ideal for a good crop.

Harvesting The berries are picked when mature but still green, because they lose their aroma as they ripen. In Jamaica, cultivated berries are hand-picked, dried artificially or on concrete platforms for five to ten days, then winnowed and graded by size. As they dry, the berries turn a red-brown shade.

Aroma & taste Allspice has a pleasantly fragrant aroma and the name reflects the pungent taste, which resembles a peppery compound of cloves, cinnamon and nutmeg or mace.

USES

Culinary Allspice is primarily used in the food industry: in ketchups, pickles, sausages, and in meat canning. It gives a gentle, warm flavour to cakes, jams and fruit pies. In Jamaica the spice is widely used in soups, stews and curries.

Medicinal The essential oil flavours a number of medicines. Allspice gives limited relief for intestinal and digestive disorders.

Other uses For centuries allspice has been included in pot-pourris (p.149).

Anise

Known as anise or aniseed, this spice is related botanically to caraway, cumin, dill and fennel. The aromatic, oval seeds are one of the oldest-known spices. Now grown in many parts of the world, anise is native to the Middle East and the islands of the eastern Mediterranean. The Romans introduced its seed to Tuscany. In the Middle Ages, cultivation of anise spread throughout Europe. It was used in England by the 14th century and grown in many kitchen gardens by the middle of the 16th century. The seed reached the New World with early colonists, where the Shakers grew it as a medicinal crop.

Anise has always been popular as a digestive. In ancient Rome, anise-spiced cakes were sometimes served after a rich meal to aid digestion. Aniseed was also taken as a digestive in the Middle Ages, in the form of comfits (seeds coated with sugar). Today, anise seeds are chewed whole in India to aid digestion and to sweeten the breath.

The plant has bright green feathery leaves and tufts of white flowers.

Seeds These vary in colour from green-grey to yellow-brown. Oval in shape with ten lighter-coloured ridges, the seeds often have bits of stalk attached.

Ground anise Like many other spices, aniseed quickly loses its flavour and aroma when ground. Buy in small quantities and grind as needed.

Essential oil Sometimes used instead of liquorice root to give foods a liquorice flavour. Most of the oil distilled for medicinal purposes comes from Russia.

Anise sweets The flavour of anise is popular in sweets and confectionery.

Pernod A wide range of drinks and liqueurs is prepared with aniseed.

CULTIVATION

Distribution The spice is cultivated commercially in the southern republics of the USSR, in Turkey, Spain, France, Germany and India.

Appearance & growth An elegant annual, anise grows to a height of 30-40cm (12-15in) and is easily grown from seed in a light rich soil.

Harvesting The plants are pulled up just before the fruit ripens, and piled up to dry. Then they are threshed

and the seeds are dried on trays in light shade outdoors or in moderate heat indoors.

Aroma & taste Both smell and taste are slightly sweet and distinctly liquorice-like.

USES

Culinary In Europe, anise is widely used as a cake and biscuit spice, and in the Middle East and India it is added to soups, stews and sometimes breads. Around the

Mediterranean, the oil from the seeds is much in demand for the manufacture of anise-flavoured aperitifs and liqueurs.

Medicinal Anise is considered a mild expectorant and added to cough mixes and lozenges. It is also used to mask the taste of bitter drugs.

Other uses In India, anise water is used as a cologne.

Pepper & long pepper

THE SPICE MOST WIDELY USED in the West, and once so highly valued that it was traded ounce for ounce for gold, pepper is native to the monsoon forests of the Malabar coast in southwest India. Black pepper is the unripe fruit of the vine P*iper nigrum*. White, green and pink peppercorns are berries from the same vine, picked at different stages of maturity. P*iper longum*, or long pepper, is a related plant known in Sanskrit as *pippali*, from which our name pepper derives.

Long pepper spread throughout southern Asia before black pepper and was probably the first variety of pepper to reach the Mediterranean. In the fourth century BC, the Greek philosopher Theophrastus described both long and black pepper, and by the first century AD, the Roman historian Pliny reported that long pepper was worth almost four times as much as black. In AD 176, the Romans imposed customs duty on long and white pepper, but black was exempt. Pepper spread from Rome into the Empire, and by the time the Goths laid siege to the city in AD 408, they demanded 3,000 lb of pepper, as well as gold and silver, as their tribute.

For centuries, pepper was negotiable as currency in the East and the West. The Chinese called pepper "fagara of the Westerners" and regarded it as an exotic substitute for their own pepper-like spice. During the Middle Ages, pepper was sometimes used to pay rents, dowries and taxes, and was so expensive that the English took to using a herb substitute to flavour their food. The demand for pepper provided the main impetus for the discovery by the explorer Vasco da Gama of a sea route to the East.

The flowers are replaced by clusters of green berries, which turn red as they ripen.

Fresh These strings of fresh green berries are sometimes available in supermarkets in the West. Add a few whole berries to duck dishes and to cream and butter sauces.

Black peppercorns *Green fruits are picked and piled in heaps to ferment for a few days, then sun-dried; they shrivel and turn hard and black. The peppercorns are more wrinkled than the other types.*

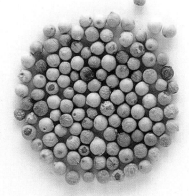

White peppercorns *Ripe berries are soaked in water, the outer skin is rubbed off, and the grey inner peppercorns are dried until they turn creamy-white.*

Ground black pepper *The aroma of pepper disappears quickly, so it is best to grind peppercorns as needed.*

Ground white pepper *Specks of white pepper are more attractive in creamy sauces than black.*

Pepper mill *For everyday kitchen use, try mixing black and white peppercorns in a pepper mill.*

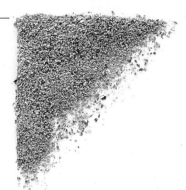

Ground green pepper
*Seldom available commercially;
prepare at home.*

Green peppercorns Immature pepper,
these are preserved by freeze-drying or
packing in brine or vinegar.

Peppers in brine Rinse the
berries and add either whole
or crushed to the dish.

Ground schinus molle

Schinus molle These berries are often sold
as pink peppercorns. They have a brittle
outer shell enclosing a small seed and taste
aromatic, rather than pungent.

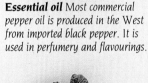

Essential oil Most commercial
pepper oil is produced in the West
from imported black pepper. It is
used in perfumery and flavourings.

Ground mixed pepper

Mixed peppercorns

Long pepper About 2.5cm (1in) long,
resembling small, stiff, grey-black catkins.

CULTIVATION
Distribution India, Malaysia
(Sarawak) and Indonesia (Sumatra)
are the main producers, closely
followed by Brazil. Long pepper
grows wild from the foothills of the
Himalayas to southern India.

Appearance & growth Pepper is a
perennial vine with dark green
leaves and spikes of white flowers.
The vine takes seven to eight years
to reach full maturity, and continues
to bear fruit for 15-20 years. It is
trained up posts or the trees grown
for shade in coffee plantations. Long
pepper, also a tropical vine, has
similar leaves and flowers.

Harvesting The berries of *piper nigrum*
are harvested over 2-3 months in
the spring and summer. Peppercorns - dried berries - are graded by
size: the larger the berry, the better
the quality. Long pepper berries are
gathered when green, then dried in
the sun.

Aroma & taste Pepper has a warm,
woody smell that is fresh, pungent
and agreeably aromatic. White
pepper tastes hotter and less subtle
than black; green pepper is not as
hot and has a clean, fresh taste.
Long pepper resembles black in
taste, but is slightly less pungent,
with a hint of sweetness.

USES
Culinary Pepper is neither sweet nor
savoury, just pungent, and can
therefore be used in both types of
dish. It is so popular that it has given
its name to a wide range of dishes.
   Use peppercorns whole to flavour
stocks and cooking liquids; crush
them coarsely when adding to dry-
spice mixtures or marinades.
   Long pepper is always used whole
and is seldom found outside the Far
East, where it is used as a cooking
spice and in pickles and preserves.

Medicinal Pepper is said to help
relieve flatulence and to have
diuretic properties.

Cubeb

Nᴀᴛɪᴠᴇ ᴛᴏ ᴊᴀᴠᴀ and other Indonesian islands, cubebs are the unripe fruits of a plant belonging to the pepper family. They are also known as tailed pepper because of their appearance. The herbalist John Parkinson describes them as "small berries somewhat sweete, no bigger than pepper cornes but more rugged or crested not so blacke nor solid ... and having each a small short stalke at them like a taile".

Used in ancient China as a medicine, cubebs reached the West through Arab traders and were valued as a medicine and a spice. They remained in quite common use until the end of the 17th century. In his *Theatrum Botanicum* of 1640, Parkinson reports that the sale of cubebs was forbidden by the king of Portugal in order to promote the sale of black pepper. By the 19th century, cubebs were virtually unobtainable. Today, medical herbalists are the most likely source of the spice.

The fruits, which are the spice, grow in clusters.

Berries Dark brown in colour, the tailed berries have a wrinkled, leathery skin. They can be up to 6mm in diameter.

Split berries When split open, some of the berries have a small dark or white seed; others are hollow.

Ground cubeb The powdered spice can be used instead of ground pepper.

Essential oil An ingredient in some throat lozenges.

Ras el hanout One of the spice mixtures in which whole cubebs are used.

CULTIVATION

Distribution Although cultivated commercially in parts of Indonesia and in Sri Lanka, often in coffee plantations, most cubebs are gathered from the wild.

Appearance & growth The cubeb plant is a perennial climber with smooth, pointed leaves and small, white flowers that grow in spikes.

Harvesting The fruits are gathered before they ripen, when still green.

They are then dried in the sun to a deep brown-black.

Aroma & taste Cubebs have a warm, turpentine-like aroma. The taste is aromatic - Parkinson called it hot and glowing - but it is also somewhat bitter. It is closer to allspice than to pepper.

USES

Culinary Today, cubebs are still used in spice mixtures such as ras el hanout (pp.96-7) and in Indonesian

cuisine. They can be added to any dish in place of allspice and are particularly suited to meat and vegetable dishes.

Medicinal Cubebs have been used as a medicine since antiquity and are still valued in the East. They help clear phlegm and are an ingredient in preparations for respiratory complaints. Cubebs also have antiseptic properties.

Sumac

T HE DECORATIVE SUMAC BUSH grows wild throughout the Middle East and bears
spikes of tart, red berries. These are dried to a deep brick colour and used,
whole or ground, in the cooking of the region. They give a fruity, sour note to a
dish and are used in a similar way to lemon juice or vinegar in the West. Sumac
is especially popular in Lebanon, where most homes have a constant supply.

The Romans used sumac as a souring agent before lemons were available in
Europe. North American Indians used the red berries of a related shrub, *Rhus
glabra*, to make a sour drink. A little-known spice in the West, sumac can be
bought from some Middle Eastern shops, where it is usually sold as a deep
purple-red coarse powder.

*The leaves turn a shade
of red in autumn.*

Berries *These vary in colour
from brick to brown- or
purple-red, depending on the
area they come from.*

Seeds *Small brown seeds from
the centre of the berries.*

Ground *In an airtight jar,
ground sumac will keep its
flavour for several months.*

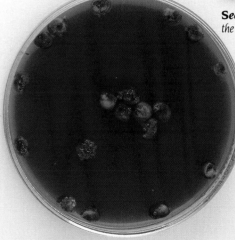

Soaked berries
*If the berries are used
whole in recipes, they
are cracked and
soaked in water for
20 minutes, then
pressed well to extract
all the juice, which is
used as part of the
cooking liquid.*

Zahtar *A Middle Eastern spice blend of
ground sumac, roasted sesame seeds and
powdered dried thyme (p.96).*

CULTIVATION
Distribution Sumac grows wild in
Sicily, and on the high plateau lands
running from Turkey eastwards to
the Caspian Sea and through the
Arab lands to the south.

Appearance & growth The spice
comes from a bush, which grows to
about 3m (10ft) on sparsely wooded
uplands. The plant bears white
flowers, which are followed by
clusters of small red berries. It
thrives on rocky mountains: the
higher it grows, the better the fruit.

Harvesting The berries are picked
just before they ripen fully. They are
dried before use. In early autumn
huge piles of drying sumac stalks
with strings of tightly clustered
berries can be seen in the villages of
Anatolia in Turkey.

Aroma & taste Sumac has little
aroma, but its taste is pleasantly
sour and astringent, without
being sharp.

USES
Culinary Widely used in the Middle
East: the Lebanese and Syrians

sprinkle sumac on fish; the Iraquis
and Turks add it to salads; and the
Iranians and Georgians season
kebabs with it. Sumac goes well with
lentils, in a stuffing for chicken, with
raw onions and mixed with yogurt.

Medicinal In Middle Eastern
countries, sumac is made into a sour
drink that is given to relieve mild
stomach disorders.

Other uses The bark and leaves of
the tree are used as a dye and for
dressing leather.

Sesame

B ELIEVED TO BE the oldest plant grown for its oil, sesame has long been cultivated in Africa and Asia. The seeds contain about 50 percent fixed oil, which is excellent for cooking and does not turn rancid in heat. Sesame probably originated from Africa, though claims have been made for Iran, India and Indonesia. It has been used in China for around 2,000 years, yet, because it is not native, it is still called "foreign hemp". Sesame is one of the medicinal plants listed in the Ebers papyrus (*c*.1550 BC), and excavations in eastern Turkey have found evidence of oil being extracted from the seeds dating back to 900-700 BC. On his travels, Marco Polo noted that the Persians used sesame oil for cooking because they had no olive oil. Sesame reached the New World in the 17th and 18th centuries with African slaves, who called it *benne*.

The plant has variable, hairy leaves and white or pink flowers.

Brown seeds Oval in shape, these beige, unhulled seeds have a characteristic nutty flavour.

Creamy white seeds *These small flat seeds are the most common. They are quite shiny and slippery and not very hard.*

Black seeds *These are popular in Chinese and Japanese cooking.*

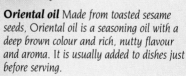

"Western" oil *A polyunsaturated oil, used in margarines and as a cooking oil.*

Halva *Probably the best-known sweetmeat made with sesame.*

Oriental oil *Made from toasted sesame seeds, Oriental oil is a seasoning oil with a deep brown colour and rich, nutty flavour and aroma. It is usually added to dishes just before serving.*

Tahina *This paste, made from the ground seeds, is used in the Middle East and eastern Mediterranean for dressings, to flavour vegetables and fruit dishes, and as a salad, mixed with garlic and lemon juice, and sometimes ground nuts.*

CULTIVATION

Distribution The main producers are China, India, Mexico, Guatemala, and the southwest United States.

Appearance & growth An annual grown from seed, the plant reaches 1-1.5m (3-5ft). The colour of the seeds depends on the variety.

Harvesting The lower pods on the plant ripen first, so harvesting begins when the higher pods are still green. The plants are cut, then threshed, dried and cleaned.

Aroma & taste Sesame seeds have no essential oil, so they are not aromatic. The taste is mild, sweet and nutty, particularly after roasting. Black seeds have a stronger, more earthy taste than the lighter ones.

USES

Culinary In Western and Middle Eastern cooking, sesame seeds are used rather like poppy seeds to decorate and flavour breads, cakes and confectionery, such as halva. The Chinese coat foods with sesame before cooking to give them a crunchy texture; sesame prawn balls

and toast are popular Chinese appetizers. In Japan, the seeds are toasted and sprinkled on rice and other dishes, and are used in dressings for salads and vegetables. Oriental sesame paste is used in dressings for noodles, rice and vegetables.

Medicinal The seeds and their oil are slightly laxative.

Other uses Sesame oil is used in the manufacture of soap and cosmetics; in India it is traditionally rubbed on the body as an anointing oil.

Tamarind

T HE DARK BROWN, bean-shaped pod of the tamarind tree has been cultivated in India for centuries, hence its other name, Indian date. Popular with the Arabs in the Middle Ages, it was probably introduced to Europe by the Crusaders. In Tudor times tamarind was known in England for its thirst-quenching properties. In the 17th century it was taken by the Spaniards to the West Indies, where it is cultivated today.

Tamarind is generally sold in sticky brown-and-white blocks of partly dried, broken pods and pulp, or as a concentrate. Whole pods can sometimes be bought in Indian shops. It is used as a souring agent in India and Southeast Asia, much as lemon and lime juice are used in the Middle East and the West. Tamarind is particularly good with fish and poultry dishes.

The fruits are curved pods, which turn dark brown when ripe.

Slices *Dried pieces of tamarind; soak in water to extract the flavour.*

Block *A fibrous mass. To make tamarind water, soak a small piece of the block in 300ml (¹/₂pt) of hot water for about ten minutes, and squeeze out the sour brown juice with your fingers. Strain afterwards.*

Pods *The brown pods have a brittle shell and grow up to 10cm (4in) long. Inside is a fleshy pulp, which can contain as many as ten seeds.*

Sugar-coated balls *These have a mild flavour and virtually no smell. Soak in a little water before use.*

Concentrate *A thick, dark paste with a smell resembling molasses and a distinct sharp, acidic taste.*

CULTIVATION

Distribution Thought to be native to East Africa and perhaps southern Asia, the tamarind tree grows wild throughout India, and is cultivated widely in the tropics.

Appearance & growth An evergreen, the tamarind tree bears pale green oval leaves and small clusters of yellow flowers with red veins. Trees are grown from seed or cuttings, and need little attention.

Harvesting The pods may be picked when immature, but usually they are fully ripe and cracked, revealing the red-brown pulp.

Aroma & taste Tamarind has a slightly sweet aroma and a pleasantly sour, fruity flavour.

USES

Culinary In India tamarind is used in curries; *sambhars* (spiced lentil and vegetable stews); *rasams* (highly seasoned lentil soups) and chutneys. In Thailand it makes hot and sour soups; in the West Indies, cooling drinks are made from tamarind syrup. In Jamaica the sweetly acidic fruit is used in rice dishes and stews and to make desserts. Pectin is extracted from the fruit for use in jam and jelly making. In the West, tamarind is imported for condiments such as Worcestershire sauce.

Medicinal Tamarind is a mild laxative, and is used in India as a traditional treatment for dysentery and bowel disorders. Rich in vitamins, tamarind is reputed to be good for the liver and kidneys.

Other uses The leaves of the tree yield red and yellow dyes.

Ajowan

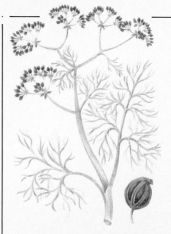

The plant resembles wild parsley.

AJOWAN IS CULTIVATED primarily for its essential oil, the main ingredient of which is thymol, a germicide and antiseptic. Native to southern India, ajowan is an annual related to caraway and cumin, although its taste is quite different, having a close affinity to thyme. Sometimes called lovage, ajwain or carom in Indian recipes, ajowan is a popular spice throughout India, particularly in savoury dishes and snacks, although it is probably used as much for medicinal purposes as for cooking. Ajowan seeds are found in most Indian households, where they are taken to relieve indigestion and flatulence, which may partly explain why they are often cooked with pulses. Ajowan goes well with fish, and the seeds are sometimes added to curries. In the West the spice is available from Indian grocery shops.

Seeds The curved and ridged oval seeds look similar to celery seeds, but their colour varies from light brown to purple-red.

Ground Once crushed, the seeds are highly aromatic. Thyme or lovage can be used as substitutes in recipes.

Paratha Ajowan seeds are often added to Indian breads.

Bombay mix A popular Indian snack of mixed nuts, pulses and crisp sticks flavoured with ajowan and other spices.

CULTIVATION

Distribution India is the main supplier of ajowan, but it is also grown in Afghanistan, Pakistan, Iran and Egypt.

Appearance & growth An annual that grows to 30-60cm (1-2ft) in height, ajowan thrives in well-drained soil in a sunny location.

Harvesting Once the seeds have ripened, they are dried and then threshed. The seeds fall off easily if bunches of ajowan are hung upside down in a dry atmosphere, an effective process with most spices in the same family as parsley.

Aroma & taste Until crushed, the seeds have little aroma, but even pressing them lightly in the palm of the hand releases a crude smell of thyme. The taste is hot, bitter and stinging on the tongue if they are sampled alone, but cooked with other ingredients ajowan adds a more subdued flavour of thyme.

USES

Culinary Ajowan seems to have a natural affinity with starchy foods and in southwestern Asia it is widely used in breads and savoury pastries, with root vegetables and with pulses. Many pickles include ajowan. If substituting it for thyme, use less ajowan since it has a much stronger flavour.

Medicinal Besides its use to control flatulence and indigestion, ajowan is prescribed for colic, diarrhoea and other bowel disorders, and in the treatment of asthma. The essential oil is an important antiseptic used, among other things, in mouthwashes and toothpastes.

Fenugreek

A MEDICINAL HERB and popular flavouring since antiquity, fenugreek is native to the eastern Mediterranean. The plant's Latin name, *foenum-graecum*, means Greek hay; *trigonella* refers to the triangular shape of its pale yellow flowers. The Egyptians made a paste from the seeds, which they applied to the body to reduce fever, and fenugreek was one of the spices used in fumigation and embalming. For the Romans, fenugreek was important as cattle fodder; 1,000 years later it was one of the plants grown throughout Europe in the imperial gardens of Charlemagne.

Fenugreek restores nitrogen to the soil and is still used today in the East as cattle fodder. It provides a good source of protein, vitamins and minerals, and is particularly useful in a vegetarian diet.

The whole plant emits a spicy odour when touched.

Seeds *The seeds are yellow-brown with a deep furrow running diagonally across one side. They are smooth and hard, rather like tiny pebbles, about 3-5mm long.*

Crushed *Lightly roast the seeds before crushing to bring out their flavour.*

Ground *It is best to grind fenugreek at home since commercial powder is often bitter and pungent.*

Sprouted *The seeds can be sprouted like mustard and cress to make an excellent salad green.*

Dried leaves *In India and parts of the Middle East, the leaves (methi) are cooked, often in combination with starchy root vegetables. They have a bitter taste and strong aroma.*

Çemen *In Turkey and Armenia, ground fenugreek, red pepper and garlic are blended to coat pastırma, the delicious dried meat of the region.*

CULTIVATION

Distribution Widely grown around the Mediterranean, and in India, Pakistan, Morocco, France and Argentina.

Appearance & growth Fenugreek is a robust annual that grows to 60cm (2ft) in height and thrives in mild climates with low rainfall. Its narrow, beaked seed pods are 10-12cm (4-5in) long, and each contains 10-20 seeds.

Harvesting When the seeds are ripe, the plants are pulled up and dried.

The seeds are then threshed and dried further.

Aroma & taste The strong, aromatic smell of fenugreek is similar to that of celery or lovage, and dominates commercial curry powder.

Uncooked fenugreek tastes bitter, astringent and very disagreeable; it is often lightly dry roasted before use to mellow the flavour.

USES

Culinary Fenugreek is combined with other spices in many Indian dishes and pickles. It is an ingredient

of sambhar powder (pp.82-3) as well as curry powder (pp.80-1). In Egypt and Ethiopia, fenugreek is used in bread; it is also a constituent of Ethiopian Berbere (pp.92-3).

Medicinal Fenugreek is an important source of diosgenin, which is used in the synthesis of sex hormones and oral contraceptives.

Other uses Formerly used as a yellow dye.

Vanilla

USED FOR CENTURIES as a flavouring by the Aztec Indians in Mexico, vanilla was offered as a tribute to the Aztec emperor by his subject tribes. In 1520 one of the Spanish *conquistadores*, Bernal Diaz, recorded that ground vanilla was added to the chocolate drink served to the emperor Montezuma.

The Spaniards imported the fruit and gave it its name: vanilla is the diminutive of *vaina*, meaning pod. By the second half of the 16th century, vanilla was being used to flavour chocolate in Europe, but Mexico kept a monopoly on its production until 1841, when a method of artificially fertilizing the plant by hand was developed, enabling it to be grown elsewhere.

Real vanilla is expensive, so cheap imitations are commonplace. Artificial vanillin was first produced in 1874, and this inferior synthetic, which flavours many commercial products, now meets about 90 percent of world demand.

The vine bears large waxy yellow-green flowers and long narrow pods with small seeds.

Vanilla pods These are dark brown, narrow, long, somewhat wrinkled, waxy and supple. The best pods are coated with white crystals of a natural substance called vanillin, which gives them their characteristic flavour and aroma.

Inferior pod Lighter or red-brown in colour, poor-quality pods are hard and dry and lack aroma. Vanillin frosting is not hard to fake, so inferior pods are sometimes "upgraded".

Split pod Inside, the pods contain numerous tiny black seeds embedded in dark aromatic oil.

Pod in alcohol Vanilla extract and essence are prepared by macerating beans in alcohol; essence usually has added syrup.

Vanilla essence This is very concentrated, so use it sparingly. Vanilla extract has a milder flavour; add this half a teaspoonful at a time.

Vanilla sugar Keep a vanilla pod in a jar of sugar; it flavours beautifully and lasts for years.

CULTIVATION

Distribution Native to Central America. Mexico, Puerto Rico, Madagascar and Réunion are the main producers and exporters. Despite the wide use of synthetic vanilla, the natural vanilla market is buoyant and vanilla provides an important source of revenue. The United States, France and Germany are the main importers.

Appearance & growth The fleshy vanilla vine grows in tropical lowland forests and climbs trees to a height of 10-15m (33-50ft); when cultivated it is trained to a convenient height for pollinating and harvesting.

Harvesting The pods are picked unripe and there is a lengthy and complicated curing process, which helps to explain vanilla's high cost.

Aroma & taste A rich, mellow, perfumed tobacco-like aroma is matched by a mellow, fragrant, sweet taste. Synthetic vanilla has a more obvious, heavy aroma and a rather disagreeable aftertaste. Compare the two and you won't use synthetic again.

USES

Culinary Ice cream, custards, puddings, cakes and chocolate rely on vanilla for their flavour. Much of the flavouring used is synthetic, although vanilla pods are now easier to buy than they used to be, and on the Continent natural vanilla has always been important. It is well worth buying the whole pods: they can be used many times over, and even after soaking in milk or a sauce, just wash, dry and store.

Other uses A concentrated form is used in perfumery.

Fagara / Sichuan pepper

CALLED BY MANY NAMES - anise pepper, Sichuan pepper, Chinese pepper, flower pepper (from its Cantonese name *fahjiu*) - the spice is not in any way related to our familiar black and white pepper. Many kinds of fagara have been used in cooking and in medicine in China, India and Japan for centuries. The Sichuan variety is regarded as the best.

Fagara is the red-brown dried berry of the Chinese variety of the small prickly ash tree. With cassia and ginger, it is one of the oldest established spices in China. In ancient times fagara was used to flavour wines and foods offered to the gods; it is said that the eighth-century emperor Te Tsung took fagara and curds in his tea, and the poet Han-shan of the same period wrote about "roast duck tinctured with fagara and salt". Fagara became a standard table condiment in China and at one time it was fashionable to give sachets of the spice as a gift to friends.

The Chinese prickly ash is covered in sharp spikes.

Whole *The red-brown berries are about 4-5mm long, and have a rough, prickly exterior. They are hollow and split open and sometimes have bits of stalk still attached.*

Seeds *Discard any loose black seeds, or seeds in the centre of the berries; they are very bitter.*

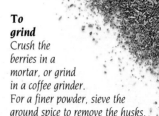

To grind *Crush the berries in a mortar, or grind in a coffee grinder. For a finer powder, sieve the ground spice to remove the husks.*

Seasoned salt *From a recipe in Asian Ingredients by Bruce Cost. It is made by roasting two tablespoons fagara, three tablespoons sea salt and one teaspoon white peppercorns in a dry pan until the fagara smokes, then grinding all to a coarse powder.*

Xanthoxylum piperitum SANSHO

Also confusingly called Japanese pepper, sansho is closely related to fagara. The berry of the Japanese variety of the prickly ash is dried and ground to an aromatic, tangy, coarse powder. One of the few spices used in Japanese cooking, sansho is used principally to counter the taste of fatty foods; the Japanese sprinkle it on food, much as we do pepper.

CULTIVATION
Distribution This variety of the prickly ash grows wild throughout China, flourishing on hill slopes.

Appearance & growth A feathery-leaved deciduous tree or shrub, which has stout, sharp prickles and bears small red berries.

Harvesting The berries are harvested in autumn and dried in the sun until they split open.

Aroma & taste The berries have a pronounced spicy-woody aroma, and a numbing, rather than a sharp or bitter, taste.

USES
Culinary Fagara is an excellent seasoning for poultry and meat, and in China it is used to flavour dishes such as Sichuan crispy duck and Pang Pang chicken, a peppery dish, served chilled with cucumber and spring onions. The ground berries are an essential ingredient in

Chinese five-spice powder (pp.72-3). For more flavour, dry roast the berries in a heavy pan to release their aromatic oils before using whole, crushed or ground. Fagara will smoke as it gets hot, so keep the heat low and discard any berries that have blackened.

Medicinal In medieval Chinese medicine, the berries and their seeds were widely used; one variety of fagara was taken as a cure for dysentery.

Ginger

ONE OF THE OLDEST and most important spices, ginger has been cultivated in tropical Asia for over 3,000 years. It was widely used in ancient India and China, although it is uncertain in which of these countries ginger originates. It was one of the first spices to reach the Mediterranean, probably traded by the Phoenicians, and was known in ancient Egypt, Greece and Rome. The first-century Roman epicure, Apicius, recommends it in sauces for meat and chicken, with dried peas and lentils, and in aromatic salt. By the ninth century ginger was so widespread throughout Europe that it was set out on the table as salt and pepper are today.

The rhizomes are easy to transport, so ginger was the first Oriental spice to be widely introduced elsewhere. The Arabs took it to East Africa in the 13th century; the Portuguese to West Africa and the Spaniards to the West Indies early in the 16th century. Today it grows almost everywhere in tropical regions.

Ginger is known for its ability to warm people. In his *Theatrum Botanicum* of 1640, the herbalist John Parkinson wrote: "The properties of ginger are to warme a cold stomacke, and to helpe digestion". Ginger spiced up the English language too: "to ginger up" means to liven up. The term "ginger" is applied to people with red hair because of their alleged hot temperament.

Long, slender stalks and leaves grow from the creeping root.

Fresh ginger *The fresh rhizome is knobbly, off-white or buff-coloured, and often branched. It should feel firm and the pale yellow flesh should not be too fibrous. Fresh ginger is also known as green ginger.*

Dried ginger *The dried and cracked roots are sometimes called races. These are sold in pieces and are best bruised before using.*

Preserved ginger Tender pieces of ginger in syrup, often called stem ginger. It is exported from China, Hong Kong and Australia. In the past, it was sold in pottery or china jars.

Ground ginger This is widely used in European baking, in breads, biscuits, cakes and confectionery, as well as in Oriental spice blends.

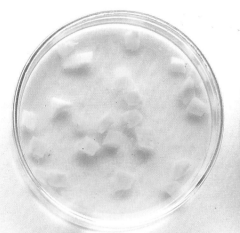

Ginger oil *This flavours wines, beers and cordials. It is also given to relieve flatulence and indigestion.*

Ginger tea *Made by infusing dried or fresh root in boiling water for five minutes; excellent for clearing head colds.*

Ginger wine *A popular and warming drink in cold weather.*

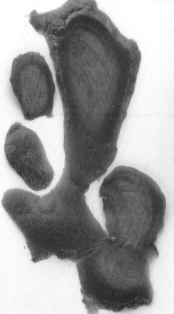

Pickled ginger *Wafer-thin slices of pickled ginger - pink* sushoga *or red* beni-shoga *- are served with Japanese dishes, especially* sushi.

Crystallized ginger *Pieces of ginger are candied, dried, and rolled in sugar.*

Gingerbread man *Gingerbread has been popular since the Middle Ages.*

CULTIVATION

Distribution A native of the tropical forests of Southeast Asia, ginger is now widely grown in the West Indies, Hawaii, Africa and northern Australia. China and India are the biggest producers, but Jamaican ginger is said to be the best.

Appearance & growth The ginger plant grows up to 1m (3ft) tall on partly shaded slopes. It has narrow pointed leaves and small yellow, purple-lipped flowers resembling irises. The hard, knobbly rhizome is about 2cm (³/₄in) in diameter.

Harvesting Rhizomes for use fresh or preserved can be dug up five to six months after planting, while still tender. For fresh ginger, the rhizomes are washed, and dried for a day or two. They can then be stored for several months in a controlled atmosphere. Ginger to be preserved is soaked in brine for a few days, then cold water. After this, it is boiled in water, then syrup.

Ginger intended for use dried is usually prepared from rhizomes harvested eight to ten months after planting. By this time, the rhizomes have become more fibrous and pungent. They are peeled or soaked in boiling water before drying.

Aroma & taste Ginger has a warm aroma with a fresh woody note and sweet, rich undertones. Its flavour is hot and slightly biting.

USES

Culinary China and most other Asian countries use fresh ginger, often with garlic. Both fresh and dried are common in India. In Arab and Western cooking ginger is mostly used dried, but fresh is now more widely available, and its use is increasing.

Ginger has numerous applications in sweet and savoury cooking. It is an essential ingredient of curry powder and other spice blends, and is found in gingerbread, biscuits, cakes, puddings, pickles and many Asian vegetable dishes. Ginger beer and wine are popular drinks and in the past, ginger was added to wine.

Medicinal The Greek physician Dioscorides recommended ginger for the stomach and as an antidote to poisons. It is still widely used in Asian medicine as a digestive aid. Ginger tea is a warming drink thought to improve the circulation. It also eases travel sickness, as does crystallized ginger.

Citrus hystrix
Kaffir lime

THE SMALL KAFFIR LIME TREE grows in Southeast Asia. The rind of the fruit and the leaves are used in Thai and Indonesian cooking, and in the West can be bought fresh or dried from Oriental shops. The leaves have a clean, floral aroma, rather like lemon verbena, and give a distinctive taste to chicken and fish dishes. Lemon grass, lemon or ordinary lime peel can if necessary be used as a substitute, but the flavour will not be the same.

Fruit *Pear-shaped, bumpy and wrinkled. The bitter rind is used in cooking.*

Leaves *The leaves have an unusual double form - as if two leaves have grown end to end.*

Dried leaves *A less fragrant substitute if fresh leaves are not available.*

Languas officinarum / Alpinia officinarum
Lesser galangal

LESSER GALANGAL is widely used in Southeast Asian cooking (p.45). Another form of galangal, kempferia galangal, is generally found dried and sliced in the West. It has a refreshing but strong taste, and should therefore be used sparingly.

Lesser galangal *A small rhizome with a reddish-brown skin and lighter-coloured interior.*

Kaempferia galanga
Kempferia galangal

Kempferia galangal *The rhizome resembles a cluster of fingers.*

Mangifera indica
Mango powder (A*mchoor*)

NATIVE TO INDIA, mango is one of the most popular tropical fruits, prized for its use in chutneys and pickles. The spice *amchoor* is made from tart, unripe mangoes, which are sliced and sun-dried, then ground to a powder and used as a souring agent. It is most commonly used in northern Indian vegetarian cooking, and gives a tangy, sour taste to stir-fried vegetables, stuffings for breads and pastries, and soups. In the West, the powder can be bought in most Indian shops.

Powder
The sand-coloured lumpy powder has little smell, but a sharp, acidic taste, similar to lemon or lime.

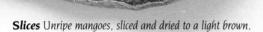
Slices *Unripe mangoes, sliced and dried to a light brown.*

Murraya koenigii
Curry leaf

CURRY LEAVES COME from a small ornamental tree that grows wild in the foothills of the Himalayas and in southern India and Sri Lanka. It is cultivated in many Indian gardens. The small leaves of this plant are used extensively in Indian cooking, particularly in vegetarian dishes. They give off a distinct curry-like odour when bruised.

Dried leaves *These have virtually no flavour - a handful of dried leaves is needed to give anything like the flavour and aroma of a stalk of fresh leaves.*

Fresh leaves *The small mid-green leaves are usually attached to the stalk. Add the whole stalk to the dish and remove before serving.*

Pandanus odoratissimus
Screwpine

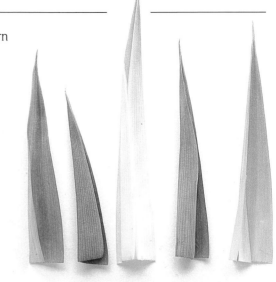

T HE SCREWPINE TREE grows in the tropical swamps of southern Asia, and bears narrow, shiny, sword-like leaves. These are used as a flavouring in Malay, Thai and Indonesian cooking, particularly in rice dishes and puddings. In the West, the leaves can be bought fresh from Oriental shops; store them in the refrigerator - they will keep for a week or two. Dried leaves are sold cut into short lengths; their · flavour is less fragrant than that of the fresh.

Screwpine flowers yield an essence, sold as kewra water or essence, which is used in India to flavour meat and poultry dishes and pilafs.

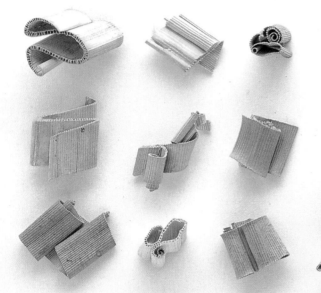

Dried leaves Add directly to the dish.

Fresh leaves *The long, thin leaves are added directly to the dish or are sometimes cooked first in a syrup, which is then strained off and added to the dish. They colour food green.*

Kewra water *This has a delicate floral, rose-like perfume and flavour.*

Prunus mahaleb
Mahlab

T HE SMALL, beige-coloured oval kernels of the black cherry tree are dried and ground to flavour breads and pastries in Turkey and the Middle East. They are quite soft, and have a nutty chewiness and a bitter, rather sour, taste when sampled on their own. The kernels are not easily available in the West, but can be bought from some Middle Eastern shops. It is best to buy mahlab whole and grind as needed.

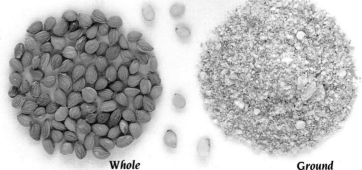

Whole   **Ground**

Punica granatum

Pomegranate

NATIVE TO SOUTHWEST ASIA, but now grown throughout the tropics and sub-tropics, the small deciduous pomegranate tree bears glossy leaves, brilliant orange-red flowers and large beige- to red-skinned fruits. These may be sweet, sweet-sour or sour, depending on the variety, but all have rather astringent juice. The seeds of the sour pomegranate are sun-dried and used as a garnish. They have a slightly sour smell and a distinctive, but subtle, sweet-sour taste. In north India, under the name *anardana*, they are ground and used as a souring agent in chutneys and curries, in fillings for breads and savoury pastries, and with braised vegetables and pulses.

Dried seeds
These look rather like red-black raisins.

Fruit
The skin is tough and inedible, but the numerous seeds inside are embedded in white, pink or red juicy flesh.

Raw seeds *In the Middle East, Turkey and Iran, these are sprinkled as a garnish on salads, pastes such as hummus or tahina and on desserts.*

Wasabia japonica

Wasabi

THIS PLANT, the "mountain hollyhock", grows only in Japan on the marshy edge of cold mountain streams. It is otherwise known as Japanese horseradish, probably because of its edible root, fierce aroma and biting, cleansing taste, although it is not related to the Western horseradish plant.

In Japan, the brownish-green skin of the root is removed, and the pale green flesh is grated finely.

Wasabi accompanies most raw fish dishes. *Sashimi* plates always have a tiny mound of grated wasabi or wasabi paste, which is mixed to taste with a soy dipping sauce. *Sushi* has a dab of wasabi paste spread between the rice and fish. Fresh wasabi is seldom available outside Japan but small tins of powder or tubes of paste can be bought in the West.

Powder *Mix wasabi powder with an equal quantity of tepid water and leave for ten minutes to develop its flavour.*

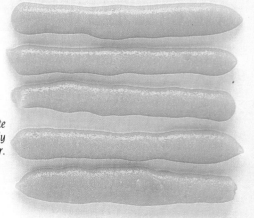

Paste *The pale green paste loses its potency more quickly than the powder.*

3

Spice mixtures

Spice blends are used extensively in many parts of the world to add a distinctive flavour to a dish. They vary in complexity and texture: some are pastes based on fresh ingredients such as chillies, others are dried mixtures of whole or ground spices. In this chapter, instructions are given for making a range of spice blends, from Asian mixtures, such as fiery Indonesian sambals and Indian garam masalas, to blends from Africa and the Middle East, and the West. The recipes can be adapted to suit your taste and the dish by varying the proportions and combinations of ingredients.

Far Eastern spice blends

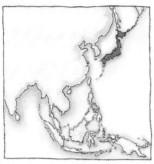

Japan

Moving east to west across Asia, spice blends increase in number and complexity. In Japan, spices are used mostly as condiments for sprinkling over dishes. China has a few more spice mixtures, but the most varied and extensive range of blends is to be found in Indonesia and Thailand.

JAPAN

The Japanese use many aromatic ingredients in their cooking, although few are spices. Those most commonly used are wasabi and sansho, which are exclusive to Japanese cuisine, chillies, mustard, ginger and sesame. All are used with moderation.

SHICHIMI TOGARASHI

This popular Japanese spice mixture translates as seven-flavour or seven-spice mix. It is used in the kitchen and as a table condiment to flavour soups, noodles and grilled meats. Proportions can be varied. The aroma is of the dried tangerine peel, with a hint of iodine from the laver; the taste is somewhat dominated by the chilli, but not overwhelmingly; and the texture is gritty. Sometimes rape seeds are substituted for the poppy seeds.

2 tsp white sesame seeds
3 tsp sansho
1 tsp small pieces of dried laver (a seaweed, called *nori* in Japan)
3 tsp flakes of dried tangerine peel
3 tsp chilli powder (togarashi)
1 tsp black sesame seeds
1 tsp poppy seeds

METHOD
Grind the white sesame seeds and sansho coarsely. Add the laver and dried tangerine peel and grind again briefly. Stir in the remaining spices and blend well. In an airtight container, the mixture will keep for 3-4 months.

GOMASIO

Goma is the Japanese name for sesame. This mixture is used as a condiment to sprinkle on rice, raw vegetables and salads. It is good on boiled potatoes, too.

5 tsp black sesame seeds
2 tsp coarse salt

METHOD
Lightly roast the sesame seeds in a dry frying pan over a medium heat for a minute or two, stirring frequently. Allow to cool, then grind them together with the salt. In an airtight jar, the blend will keep for 3-4 months.

SHICHIMI TOGARASHI

Chilli powder

Dried tangerine peel

Poppy seeds

Shichimi togarashi

GOMASIO

Black sesame seeds

Coarse salt

Gomasio

Sansho

Dried laver

White sesame seeds

Black sesame seeds

China

CHINA

The Chinese use some spice mixtures, to flavour meats and poultry and in marinades. The best-known spice blend is five-spice powder, but Chinese supermarkets also stock large bags, labelled mixed spices, which contain cassia, star anise, cardamom, dried ginger, fagara, liquorice root and cassia buds. This mixture is used in a technique common throughout China called flavour-potting, where meat is steeped in a rich spiced sauce; the sauce permeates the meat and the meat enriches the sauce. The blend has a predominantly woody smell of cassia combined with anise.

FIVE-SPICE POWDER

This mixture is used throughout southern China and Vietnam to season roast meat and poultry, and to flavour marinades. Besides the five basic ingredients, it can consist of up to two of the following spices: cardamom, dried ginger and liquorice root. The powder varies in colour, from tan to gingery-brown to amber. Star anise dominates the aroma and taste.

I tbsp star anise	
I tbsp fagara	
½ tbsp cassia or cinnamon	
I tbsp fennel seeds	
½ tbsp cloves	

METHOD
Grind all the ingredients together and use sparingly. Stored in an airtight container, five-spice powder will keep for 3-4 months.

SPICED SALT

This salt is served in small bowls and used as a dip for raw or deep-fried vegetables, roast meat and poultry.

4 tbsp coarse salt	
2 tbsp fagara	

METHOD
Dry roast the salt and fagara in a heavy frying pan over a medium heat until the fagara darkens. Cool, then grind and store in an airtight container for up to 4 months.

FIVE-SPICE POWDER

Fagara

Cardamoms

Fennel seeds

SPICED SALT

Fagara

Spiced salt

Coarse salt

Star anise

Cloves

Dried ginger

Five-spice powder

Cassia

Liquorice root

Indonesia

INDONESIA

Indonesian cooking is richly spiced with ginger, turmeric, galangal, lemon grass, aromatic leaves and herbs, but above all with chillies. In addition to the spicing used in the preparation of a dish, Indonesians make a range of relishes, based on chillies, called sambals. These are served in small dishes on the table. Some are fiercely hot because the chilli seeds have been left in; all are highly aromatic. The Indonesians use a chilli called lombok, similar to tabasco, when making sambals but other small red chillies can be substituted. Take great care when handling chillies as they can burn (pp.154-5). More sambal recipes appear on p.108.

SAMBAL OELEK

Jars of sambal can be bought in many Oriental shops and in some delicatessens, but it is quite easy to make your own, especially with a food processor. This is the most basic sambal. To make other sambals, ingredients such as trassi or blachan, a firm paste made of rotted shrimps (pp.154-5), and candlenuts are added to the mix.

METHOD
Heat a heavy frying pan and put in the chillies after 2-3 minutes. Dry roast over a medium heat for a few minutes. Cool, then chop finely and pound to a paste with the salt and sugar. The chilli seeds may be taken out, or left in if you want a really fiery relish. The sambal will keep for a week or so in a jar in the refrigerator.

250 g (8 oz) fresh red chillies
1 tsp salt
1 tsp soft brown sugar

SAMBAL BADJAK

SAMBAL OELEK

Salt

Chillies

Brown sugar

Fresh red chillies

Candlenuts

Sambal oelek

Oil

SAMBAL BADJAK

10 fresh red chillies

2 onions

5 cloves garlic

a small piece of trassi (pp.154-5)

5 candlenuts

5-10 ml (1-2 tsp) tamarind concentrate or
30-45 ml (2-3 tbsp) tamarind water (p.57)

¹/₂ tsp ground galangal

45 ml (3 tbsp) oil

1 tsp salt

1 tsp soft brown sugar

2 kaffir lime leaves

250 ml (8 fl oz) thick coconut milk, made from 125 g
(4 oz) creamed coconut dissolved in 250 ml (8 fl oz)
hot water

METHOD
Pound or process the chillies, onions, garlic, trassi and
candlenuts to a smooth paste with the tamarind and
galangal. Heat the oil and fry the paste for a few minutes,
then add the remaining ingredients and cook gently for
15-20 minutes, until the mixture thickens. Cool, and store
in a jar in the refrigerator.

Garlic

Trassi

Ground galangal

Tamarind concentrate

Onion

Kaffir lime leaves

Sambal badjak

Creamed coconut

THAILAND

Thailand has the same affection for chillies as Indonesia, and uses them with garlic, coriander, lemon grass and tamarind. Sauces called Nam prik, made with chillies (*prik*), shallots, garlic and trassi (pp.154-5), are the local equivalent of sambals. They are made quickly, with no hard and fast rules: the sauces vary from region to region and cook to cook. Nam prik is eaten with vegetables, rice and fish. More nam prik recipes appear on p.108.

Thailand

ROASTED NAM PRIK

5 cloves garlic, unpeeled
5 shallots, unpeeled
5 fresh red chillies
a small piece of trassi
1 tbsp soft brown sugar
5 ml (1 tsp) tamarind concentrate
2 tbsp peanuts

METHOD
Put the unpeeled garlic and shallots over a barbecue or in a heavy cast-iron frying pan and grill or dry fry until the skins are dark brown and the insides soft. Dry fry the chillies and the trassi wrapped in foil, until the trassi darkens and the chillies soften. Peel the garlic and shallots, chop the chillies, removing the seeds, and pound or process everything to a paste. Store for about a week in a jar in the refrigerator.

ROASTED NAM PRIK

Tamarind concentrate

Trassi

NAM PRIK for raw vegetables

4 dried red chillies
6 dried shrimps
a small piece of trassi
2 cloves garlic
30 ml (2 tbsp) fish sauce (see *Simple Thai Fish Soup*, p.112)
1 tbsp soft brown sugar
juice of one lime

METHOD
Remove the seeds from the chillies and chop. Pound or process them with the dried shrimps. Heat the trassi (see pp.154-5). Crumble it and pound with the garlic, then combine all the ingredients except the lime juice and process. Add the lime juice, a little at a time, so that the sauce remains fairly thick. Store in the refrigerator.

Dried shrimps

Brown sugar

Peanuts

Shallots

Garlic

Roasted nam prik

Fresh red chillies

Thai curry pastes

Curries are an important element in the Thai menu. They are flavoured with ferociously hot pastes made of spices and either red, green or yellow chillies, according to the ingredients used. As in India, the spice mix is prepared when needed and is not usually stored, but these pastes will keep for about a month in the refrigerator.

RED CURRY PASTE

This is used for beef and other robust dishes.

3 shallots
3 cloves garlic
2 stalks lemon grass
1 tbsp coriander seeds
1 tsp cumin seeds
1 tsp black peppercorns
10 dried red chillies
1 tbsp chopped coriander root
1 tbsp ground galangal
2 tsp grated lime peel
a small piece of trassi (pp.154-5)
salt to taste

METHOD
Chop the shallots, garlic and lemon grass. Heat a heavy frying pan and add the coriander and cumin seeds after 2-3 minutes. Dry roast until they darken, shaking the pan to prevent burning. Allow to cool, then grind to a powder with the peppercorns. Remove the seeds from the chillies and chop. Pound or process all the ingredients to a smooth paste.

VARIATION
◆ For GREEN CURRY PASTE, follow the recipe for Red curry paste, using **fresh green chillies** instead of dried red and adding 2 tbsp **chopped coriander leaves**.

Black peppercorns

Dried red chillies

Cumin seeds

Fresh green chillies

Coriander leaves

Coriander seeds

Trassi

Garlic

Shallots

RED CURRY PASTE

Grated lime peel

Salt

Ground galangal

Lemon grass

Chopped coriander root

Indian spice mixtures

South India and Sri Lanka

The blending of spices is the essence of Indian cookery; to become a good Indian cook you must first become a good *masalchi* (spice blender). The word masala means a mixture of spices, but also refers to the aromatic composition of a dish. The Western notion of having a single masala or curry powder gives little real idea of Indian cooking since there are hundreds of masalas – from different regions, for different foods, and prepared to the taste of different cooks – imparting a distinctive flavour to each dish. The most common ground blends are garam masalas, used in northern cooking, and hotter masalas or curry powders from the south. They are usually made up as required, but will keep for 3-4 months in an airtight jar.

Curry powders

In the hotter southern blends, chillies, mustard seeds, fenugreek seeds, ground turmeric and fresh curry leaves are standard ingredients. More curry mixtures appear on pp.108-9.

BASIC CURRY POWDER

This medium-hot curry blend can be used in any dish that calls for curry powder.

6 dried red chillies
25 g (1 oz) coriander seeds
2 tsp cumin seeds
½ tsp mustard seeds
1 tsp black peppercorns
1 tsp fenugreek seeds
10 fresh curry leaves
½ tsp ground ginger
1 tbsp ground turmeric

METHOD
Remove the seeds from the chillies. Dry roast the whole spices over a medium heat until they darken, stirring or shaking the pan frequently to prevent burning. Leave to cool, then grind to a powder. Dry roast the curry leaves in the pan for a few minutes, then grind and add them to the mixture with the ginger and turmeric, blending well.

VARIATION
◆ To make AROMATIC CURRY POWDER, add 1 tsp **ground cinnamon** and ¼ tsp **ground cloves** with the ginger and turmeric, and use only 2 or 3 **chillies**.

Fenugreek seeds

Black peppercorns

Dried red chillies

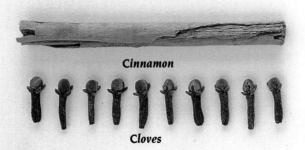

Cinnamon

Cloves

**Cumin
seeds**

Ground turmeric

**Mustard
seeds**

Ground ginger

**Coriander
seeds**

Basic curry powder

Fresh curry leaves

SAMBHAR POWDER

This hottish powder is widely used in southern Indian Brahmin cooking, which is vegetarian, to flavour pulses, braised and stewed vegetables, and sauces. The dal in the blend give it a nutty taste, and also serve as a thickening agent.

10 dried red chillies

25 g (1 oz) coriander seeds

20 g (³/₄ oz) cumin seeds

15 g (¹/₂ oz) black peppercorns

1 tsp mustard seeds

15 g (¹/₂ oz) fenugreek seeds

¹/₄ tsp ground asafoetida

1 tbsp ground turmeric

15 ml (1 tbsp) oil

25 g (1 oz) yellow split peas (*channa dal*)

25 g (1 oz) white gram beans (*urad dal*)

METHOD

Remove the seeds from the chillies. Heat a heavy frying pan and dry roast the whole spices over a medium heat for about 5 minutes. When the seeds stop spattering, add the asafoetida and turmeric and stir for a minute longer. Remove the mixture to a dry bowl, add the oil to the pan and fry the split peas and gram beans until they darken, stirring frequently to prevent burning. Add them to the bowl of spices, mix well and grind when cool. Stored in an airtight container, the powder will keep for 3-4 months.

BENGALI PANCH PHORON

This mix of whole spices comes from Bengal in the east of India, where it is used to flavour pulses and vegetable dishes. It may be put into hot oil to perfume it before other ingredients are added, or it is used to spice the ghee that is poured over a dish of lentils as it is served.

1 tbsp cumin seeds

1 tbsp fennel seeds

1 tbsp mustard seeds

1 tbsp nigella seeds

1 tbsp fenugreek seeds

METHOD

Mix all the spices together. Stored in an airtight jar, the blend will keep for 3-4 months.

SAMBHAR POWDER

White gram beans   *Yellow split peas*

Oil

Sambhar powder

BENGALI PANCH PHORON

Fenugreek seeds

Nigella seeds

Cumin seeds

Mustard seeds

Fennel seeds

Panch phoron

Fenugreek seeds

Black peppercorns

Cumin seeds

Mustard seeds

Coriander seeds

Dried red chillies

Ground turmeric

Ground asafoetida

Garam masala

Garam masala is the principal spice blend of north Indian cookery, and there are almost as many versions as there are cooks. A masala may be a simple blend of two or three spices and herbs; or it may contain a dozen or more. Some masalas, based on pepper and cloves, are quite fiery; others, using mace, cinnamon and cardamom, are aromatic.

Garam masala is always used sparingly. The spices are usually dry roasted, and may be added to the dish, whole or ground, at different stages during cooking. For pilafs, birianis and some meat dishes, the use of whole spices is traditional. For some grand Moghul dishes, dried rose petals are added to the basic mixture. More masalas appear on pp.86-7 and p.108.

North India

BASIC GARAM MASALA

Black peppercorns

Bay leaves

BASIC GARAM MASALA

This is a version of the most common type of garam masala used throughout Uttar Pradesh and the Punjab, which goes well with onion-based sauces for meats and poultry. It is a spicy, pungent blend. Change the proportions to suit your taste and the dish.

2 cinnamon sticks
3 bay leaves
40 g (1 $^1/_2$ oz) cumin seeds
25 g (1 oz) coriander seeds
20 g ($^3/_4$ oz) green or black cardamom seeds
20 g ($^3/_4$ oz) black peppercorns
15 g ($^1/_2$ oz) cloves
15 g ($^1/_2$ oz) ground mace

METHOD
Break the cinnamon sticks into pieces. Crumble the bay leaves. Heat a heavy frying pan and after 2-3 minutes put in the whole spices. Dry roast over a medium heat until the colour darkens, stirring or shaking the pan frequently to prevent burning. Leave to cool, then grind and blend with the mace. In an airtight container, the mixture will keep for 3-4 months.

Ground mace

VARIATIONS
◆ To make a mild and subtle MOGHUL MASALA, use only **green cardamoms, cinnamon, black peppercorns, mace** and a few **cloves**.

◆ For a hot GUJERATI MASALA, add **sesame seeds, fennel seeds, ajowan seeds** and **chillies**.

◆ For a mildish KASHMIRI MASALA, use **black cumin seeds, green cardamoms, black peppercorns, cloves, cinnamon, mace,** and add a little **grated nutmeg**.

◆ For a hot PARSI DHANSAK MASALA, add **fenugreek seeds, mustard seeds, chillies** and **ground turmeric**, and double the amount of **coriander seeds**.

Coriander seeds

Green cardamoms

Basic
garam
masala

Cumin seeds

Cloves

Cinnamon

CHAT MASALA

A fresh-tasting, sourish preparation used with fruit and vegetable salads. If you are unable to find the black salt (pp.154-5), simply increase the amount of coarse salt.

1 tsp cumin seeds
1 tsp black peppercorns
1/2 tsp ajowan seeds
1 tsp dried pomegranate seeds
1 tsp black salt
1 tsp coarse salt

a good pinch of crushed dried mint leaves
1/4 tsp ground asafoetida
2 tsp mango powder
1/2 tsp cayenne
1/2 tsp ground ginger

METHOD
Grind the whole spices and salt to a powder, then mix in the mint, asafoetida, mango powder, cayenne and ginger. The blend will keep for 3-4 months stored in an airtight container.

CHAT MASALA

Crushed dried mint leaves

Ground ginger

Ajowan seeds

Ground asafoetida

Cayenne

Black salt

Mango powder

Dried pomegranate seeds

Cumin seeds

GREEN MASALA

Excellent with fish or chicken.

a small piece of fresh ginger

1-2 cloves garlic

4-6 fresh green chillies

a small bunch of fresh coriander

METHOD
Peel and chop the ginger and garlic; remove the seeds from the chillies and slice. Remove the coriander stalks. Pound or blend all the ingredients to a paste with a little water.

Black peppercorns

Chat masala

Coarse salt

GREEN MASALA

Fresh ginger

Green masala

Fresh green chillies

Coriander leaves

Garlic

Other curry blends

SRI LANKAN CURRY POWDER

In Sri Lanka, spices are roasted to a deep brown before grinding; this gives much Sri Lankan food a "darker" taste than Indian dishes.

25 g (1 oz) coriander seeds
15 g (¹/₂ oz) cumin seeds
1 tbsp fennel seeds
1 tsp fenugreek seeds
a small piece of cinnamon
6 green cardamoms
6 cloves
6 fresh curry leaves
1 tsp cayenne

METHOD
Dry roast the whole spices in a heavy frying pan over a medium heat until they turn dark brown, stirring frequently to prevent burning. Leave to cool, then combine with the curry leaves and cayenne and grind to a powder. Stored in an airtight container, the blend will keep for 3-4 months.

POUDRE DE COLOMBO

Colombo is a type of curry found in the Caribbean islands of Martinique and Guadeloupe. Although called a powder, this recipe, based on one in *The Best of Caribbean Cooking* by Elisabeth Lambert Ortiz, is in fact a paste.

3 cloves garlic
2 fresh hot red chillies
¹/₈ tsp ground turmeric
1 tsp ground coriander
1 tsp ground mustard

METHOD
Peel and crush the garlic; remove the seeds from the chillies and mash. Combine all the ingredients and mix to a paste. Store in the refrigerator for up to 6 weeks.

SRI LANKAN CURRY POWDER

Fennel seeds

Coriander seeds

Sri Lankan curry powder *Cloves*

Green cardamoms

POUDRE DE COLOMBO

Garlic

Fresh red chillies

Ground mustard

Ground turmeric

Ground coriander

Poudre de Colombo

Fenugreek seeds

Cayenne

Cumin seeds

Cinnamon

Fresh curry leaves

African & Middle Eastern spice blends

Arabian Gulf

BAHARAT

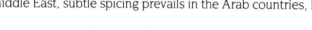

Around the Arabian Gulf, highly spiced food is still common; recipes from the region call for complex spice blends, often with chillies. Enthusiasm for rich spicing passes to North Africa, to Ethiopia and the countries of the Magreb (Morocco, Algeria and Tunisia), where food is spiced with pepper, cubebs, cumin, caraway, cinnamon and cassia, ginger and saffron. Chillies and mild peppers are common too, but not all the food is ferociously hot; many Moroccan dishes are quite delicate and subtle in their flavouring. Further south, in both East and West Africa, chillies are the dominant flavouring. Elsewhere in the Middle East, subtle spicing prevails in the Arab countries, Iran and Turkey.

Green cardamoms

Black peppercorns

Ground chilli

BAHARAT

A fiery preparation from the Gulf States, used to spice meats and vegetables. The recipe comes from *Cooking with Chillies* by Meg Jump.

¹/₂ **nutmeg, grated**
1 tbsp black peppercorns
1 tbsp coriander seeds
1 tbsp cumin seeds
1 tbsp cloves
a small piece of cinnamon
seeds from 6 green cardamoms
2 tbsp paprika
1 tsp ground chilli

METHOD
Grind all the ingredients together. The mixture will keep for 3-4 months stored in an airtight jar.

ZHUG

Ground coriander

Garlic

ZHUG

In Yemen, this is the traditional spice mix, a combination of garlic and peppers, and whatever spices the cook chooses. Use as a table condiment.

2 small mild red peppers
2-3 fresh red chillies
a handful of coriander leaves
1¹/₂ tbsp ground coriander
6 cloves garlic
seeds from 6 green cardamoms
5-10 ml (1-2 tsp) lemon juice

Green cardamoms

METHOD
Finely chop the red peppers and chillies, removing the seeds. Chop the coriander leaves. Blend or pound all the ingredients to a paste, and store in a jar in the refrigerator for up to 2 weeks.

Baharat

Grated nutmeg

Cloves

Coriander seeds

Cinnamon

Cumin seeds

Paprika

Lemon

Coriander leaves

Zhug   Fresh red chillies

Mild red peppers

· 91 ·

Ethiopia

ETHIOPIAN BERBERE

Berbere is rather like Indian masala (pp.84-7) - a complex blend of spices made to suit the dish and to the taste of the cook. Chillies, ginger and cloves are the staples; other spices vary, and some are not found outside the region. Berbere is used in traditional Ethiopian stews, called wats, and in coatings for foods to be fried. Another Ethiopian recipe appears on p.109.

10 dried red chillies
$^1/_2$ tsp coriander seeds
5 cloves
seeds from 6 green cardamoms
$^1/_4$ tsp ajowan seeds
8 allspice berries
$^1/_2$ tsp black peppercorns
$^1/_2$ tsp fenugreek seeds
a small piece of cinnamon
$^1/_2$ tsp ground ginger

METHOD

Heat a heavy frying pan and put in the chillies and other whole spices after 2-3 minutes. Dry roast over a medium heat until they darken, stirring frequently to prevent burning. Leave the spices to cool, then remove the seeds from the chillies and crumble them. Grind everything, including the ginger, to a fine powder, and store in an airtight container for up to 4 months.

Ground ginger

Allspice

Green cardamoms

Cloves

BERBERE

Dried red chillies

Coriander seeds

Black peppercorns

Berbere

Fenugreek seeds

Ajowan seeds

Cinnamon

Tunisia

TABIL

TABIL

This mixture is specific to Tunisia. Tabil means coriander, but generally refers to this blend of ingredients.

1 tbsp coriander seeds
1 1/2 tsp caraway seeds
2 cloves garlic
1 tsp dried crushed chilli

METHOD
Pound all the ingredients in a mortar, then dry in a preheated oven at 100°C, 200°F, gas 1/4 for about half an hour. When quite dry, grind to a fine powder and keep in an airtight jar for up to 4 months.

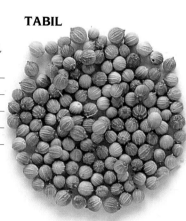

Coriander seeds

HARISSA

This fiery Tunisian chilli sauce, also found in Algeria and Morocco, is used in cooking, particularly in the vegetable or meat *tagines* (stews) that accompany couscous, and as a table condiment, rather like Indonesian sambals (pp.74-5). The sauce can be bought ready-made in small cans, but it is easy to make at home and keeps for up to 6 weeks in the refrigerator. Another Tunisian recipe appears on p.109.

50 g (2 oz) dried red chillies
2 cloves garlic
salt
1 tsp caraway seeds
1 1/2 tsp ground cumin
2 tsp coriander seeds
1 tsp crushed dried mint leaves
olive oil

METHOD
Remove the seeds and tear the chillies into pieces. Soak them in warm water until they soften (about 20 minutes). Drain, and pound or process. Crush the garlic with a little salt. Pound or blend all the ingredients to a paste, then stir in 15-30 ml (1-2 tbsp) of olive oil. Transfer to a jar, cover with a layer of olive oil, and refrigerate.

HARISSA

Olive oil

Dried red chillies

Dried
crushed chilli

Caraway seeds

Garlic

Tabil

Caraway
seeds

Crushed dried mint leaves

Ground cumin

Harissa

Salt

Coriander seeds

Garlic

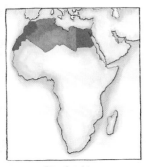

North Africa

RAS EL HANOUT

This renowned traditional Moroccan blend of 20 or more spices never fails to intrigue foreigners. *Ras el hanout* means "head of the shop", presumably because the owner mixes the blend to his own taste and to the requirements, including spending power, of the customer. The blends vary from one region to another; those from the bazaar in Fez seem to be the most complex. All contain some aphrodisiacs - *cantharides* (the shiny green Spanish fly), ash berries and monk's pepper - as well as spices and dried flowers. Ras el hanout is always sold whole and ground as required. It is considered warming, and is used with game; in rice and couscous stuffings; in lamb *tagines* (stews), such as *Mrouziya* (p.120); and in a sweetmeat of almonds, honey, butter and hashish called *el majoun*.

ZAHTAR

An aromatic mixture from North Africa, which is also found in Turkey and Jordan. It is sprinkled on meatballs or vegetables, and used as a dip. It can be mixed to a paste with olive oil and spread on bread before baking. See also the recipe for Dukka (p.109).

50 g (2 oz) sesame seeds
25 g (1 oz) ground sumac
25 g (1 oz) powdered dried thyme

METHOD
Dry roast the sesame seeds over a medium heat for a few minutes, stirring frequently. Allow to cool, then mix with the sumac and thyme. Stored in an airtight jar, the blend will keep for 3-4 months.

ZAHTAR

Zahtar

Dried thyme

Sesame seeds

Ground sumac

RAS EL HANOUT

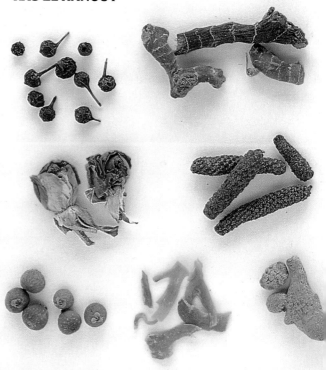

A *typical blend* This could include: *cardamom, mace, galangal, long pepper, cubebs, nutmeg, allspice, cinnamon, cloves, ginger, rose buds, lavender flowers, Spanish fly, ash berries, grains of paradise, black pepper, chufa nuts, turmeric, cassia, nigella, monk's pepper, belladonna and orris root.*

Ras el hanout

Early European spice mixtures

Europe: Italy

Spice mixtures have been used as long as spices themselves. The cooks in great medieval households had their blends of *poudre blanche* and *poudre forte*, which were usually "pointed" (sharpened and dampened) with vinegar before being added to other ingredients. Ginger seems to have been the predominating flavour, with lesser amounts of cinnamon, cloves, pepper, saffron and grains of paradise. In the 13th and 14th centuries huge quantities of powdered sugar were mixed with the spices; presumably sugar and spice went together as an indication of wealth. By the 16th century the sugar had almost disappeared; there was more variety in spice blends for different dishes. At this time, Italy led the way in cooking, and Ruperto de Nola, cook to the king of Naples, gives one of the earliest recipes for an unsweetened mixture, which he calls *Salsa comun*. This consists of: "3 parts cinnamon; 2 parts cloves; 1 part ginger; 1 part pepper with a little ground coriander and a little saffron, if wished".

SCAPPI'S SPICE MIX

Bartolomeo Scappi, the cook to Pope Pius V, specifies this blend of ingredients in his *Opera dell'Arte del Cucinare*, one of the most influential early Italian cookery books.

24 cinnamon sticks
25 g (1 oz) cloves
15 g (¹/₂ oz) dried ginger
15 g (¹/₂ oz) grated nutmeg
7.5 g (¹/₄ oz) grains of paradise
7.5 g (¹/₄ oz) saffron
15 g (¹/₂ oz) soft brown sugar

METHOD
Break the cinnamon sticks into pieces, and grind all the ingredients to a fine powder. Stored in an airtight jar, the mixture will keep for 3-4 months.

SCAPPI'S SPICE MIX

Cinnamon

Dried ginger

Brown sugar

Grains of paradise

Cloves

Grated nutmeg

Saffron

Scappi's spice mix

Later European spice mixtures

Europe: France

In the 17th century the use of large amounts of spices started to diminish; spices were more plentiful and cheaper, and although used by more people generally, were used less to exhibit status. Cookery books no longer give spice mixtures among the basic recipes at the start; the spicing needed is included in the individual recipes. In the 19th century there are more suggestions for mixed spices: Carême, the great French chef, proposes three parts peppercorns to one part of cloves, nutmeg, cinnamon, dried thyme and bayleaf, combined; and a small amount of ginger and mace. Anne Cobbett's "kitchen pepper" in the early 19th-century manual *The English Housekeeper* requires "an equal quantity of finely ground or pounded ginger, nutmeg, black pepper and allspice, cinnamon and cloves".

Today spice blends are used less widely in Europe than in the past. In France, *quatre-épices* is the most popular. In Britain, pudding spice and pickling spice are traditional mixes, still used today.

QUATRE-EPICES

The standard French "four-spice" blend is based on pepper. It is commonly used in charcuterie and in dishes that need long simmering, such as stews. Sometimes cinnamon or allspice is used in the blend.

5 tsp black peppercorns
2 tsp grated nutmeg
1 tsp cloves
1 tsp dried ginger

METHOD
Grind all the ingredients to a fine powder. In an airtight container, the mixture will keep for 3-4 months.

MELANGE CLASSIQUE

More recent French mixtures combine aromatic herbs and spices. This *mélange classique* comes from the chef's handbook *Manuel du Restaurateur*.

5 dried bay leaves
2 tsp dried thyme
1 tsp dried marjoram
1 tsp dried rosemary
2 tsp grated nutmeg
2 tsp cloves
1 tsp cayenne
1¹/₂ tsp white peppercorns
1¹/₂ tsp coriander seeds

METHOD
Crumble the bay leaves. Grind the ingredients to a fine powder and store in an airtight jar for up to 4 months.

Cloves

Quatre-épices

Dried ginger

Black peppercorns

Grated nutmeg

QUATRE-EPICES

Mélange classique

Cloves

White peppercorns

MELANGE CLASSIQUE

Dried bay leaves

Dried thyme

Coriander seeds

Dried rosemary

Cayenne

Grated nutmeg

Dried marjoram

PICKLING SPICE

An English mixture of whole spices, used for chutneys, pickled fruits and vegetables, and to spice vinegar. The spices can either be tied in a small muslin bag and removed after pickling, or added straight to the vinegar, depending on the type of pickle.

Spice merchants have their own versions; here are two given in *Law's Grocer's Manual* (1950 edition). To make manageable domestic amounts, substitute 25 g (1 oz) or even 15 g (¹/2 oz) for each pound.

Europe: British Isles

PICKLING SPICE WITH CHILLIES

"2 lb Jamaica ginger, 1³/4 lb yellow mustard seed, 1¹/2 lb Zanzibar cloves, 2¹/4 lb Indian black pepper, 1¹/2 lb birdseye or Nyasa chillies, ³/4 lb mace, ³/4 lb coriander seed, 3¹/2 lb pimento [allspice]."

PICKLING SPICE WITH CAYENNE

"2¹/2 lb mustard seed, 2 lb cayenne pods, 2¹/2 lb common black peppercorns, 1¹/2 lb white peppercorns, 1 lb small cloves, 3 lb pimento [allspice], 1¹/2 lb Jamaica ginger. Total 14 lb."

PICKLING SPICE WITH CHILLIES

Yellow mustard seeds

Cloves

Coriander seeds

Allspice

Mace

Dried ginger

Dried birdseye chillies

PUDDING SPICE

Also known as mixed spice, this English blend of sweet spices is used in cakes, biscuits and puddings. The selection of spices and the proportions used vary according to individual taste, but here is one version:

a small piece of cinnamon
1 tbsp cloves
1 tbsp mace
1 tbsp grated nutmeg
1 tbsp coriander seeds
1 tbsp allspice berries

METHOD
Grind all the spices to a fine powder. In an airtight jar, the mixture will keep for 3-4 months.

PUDDING SPICE

Black peppercorns

Coriander seeds

Cinnamon

Allspice

Cloves

Mace

Nutmeg

Pickling spice with chillies

American spice mixtures

United States

The United States is the land of commercial spice blends, invariably prepared to "secret formulae" protected by trade marks. Recipes call for apple-pie spice, barbecue blend, chicken seasoning and crab boil, all available at the local supermarket. Few cooks seem to blend their own. I have included a few versions of my own to help readers who may want to use American recipes. Make up as required.

CAJUN SEASONING

Cajun and creole cooking from Louisiana have spread throughout the States and abroad in recent years. Chillies, aromatic herbs, mustard and cumin are the main flavourings. Commercial blends tend to include onion and garlic powder, which I find have a decidedly chemical taste, so it is best to use fresh onion and garlic. This mixture is rubbed into meat or fish to be roasted or grilled, or is used to season *gumbos* (the local stews) and *jambalayas* (rice dishes). As variations, dried sage, basil or fennel can be used instead of the thyme and oregano. Other recipes from Louisiana appear on p.109.

1 fat clove garlic
$^1/_2$ small onion
1 tsp paprika
$^1/_2$ tsp ground black pepper
$^1/_2$ tsp ground cumin
$^1/_2$ tsp mustard powder
$^1/_2$ tsp cayenne
1 tsp dried thyme
1 tsp dried oregano
1 tsp salt

METHOD
Crush the garlic and onion in a mortar, and mix all the ingredients together.

Onion

Ground black pepper

Cayenne

Salt

Cajun seasoning

Garlic

Dried thyme

Paprika

Ground cumin

Mustard powder

Dried oregano

Barbecue spice mixtures

BASIC SPICE *Illustrated below*

A medium-hot blend; rub on meat before grilling.

1 tsp black peppercorns
1 tsp celery seeds
$^1/_2$ tsp cayenne
$^1/_2$ tsp dried thyme
$^1/_2$ tsp dried marjoram
2 tsp paprika
1 tbsp mustard powder
$^1/_2$ tsp salt
1 tbsp soft brown sugar

METHOD
Crush the peppercorns and celery seeds in a mortar and mix all the ingredients together.

PAPRIKA SPICE *Illustrated right*

A pungent blend, which goes well with chicken and gives it a light red colour.

a small piece of fresh ginger
1 clove garlic
1 tbsp paprika
2 tsp ground cumin

METHOD
Pound the ginger and garlic in a mortar and mix with the paprika and cumin.

JUNIPER SPICE

An aromatic blend, which is good with dense-textured fish such as monkfish, fresh tuna and swordfish, and with steaks and lamb.

2 tbsp juniper berries
1 tsp black peppercorns
6 allspice berries
3 cloves
3 dried bay leaves
$^1/_2$ tsp salt

METHOD
Grind the spices, finely crumble the bay leaves, and combine everything.

FENNEL SPICE

Fennel and lemon peel add a clean, fresh taste to this blend, which is excellent with fish.

1 clove garlic
1 tsp black peppercorns
2 tsp fennel seeds
$^1/_2$ tsp coriander seeds
1 tsp grated lemon peel
1 tsp dried thyme

METHOD
Crush the garlic in a mortar, grind the spices, and mix everything together.

BASIC SPICE

Mustard powder

Dried thyme

Cayenne

Dried marjoram

Paprika

PAPRIKA SPICE

Paprika

Ground cumin

Paprika spice

Fresh ginger

Garlic

Brown sugar

Celery seeds

Black peppercorns

Salt

Basic spice

Other spice blends

These spice mixtures, arranged by region, are either variations on the blends in the rest of this section or alternative recipes. They range from pastes and powders to a mixture of whole spices. Some are hot or medium-hot; others are mild and fragrant.

Far Eastern

SAMBAL TRASSI

a small piece of trassi (pp.154-5)
4-5 fresh red chillies
1 green chilli
1 tsp salt
1 tsp soft brown sugar
15ml (1 tbsp) lemon or lime juice

METHOD
Wrap the trassi in foil and grill until it darkens, or bake in a preheated oven at 180°C, 350°F, gas 4 for a few minutes. Remove the seeds from the chillies and chop finely. Pound or process the trassi and chillies with the other ingredients until you have a smooth paste. Store in a jar in the refrigerator for a few days.

VARIATIONS
◆ For SAMBAL ASEM, add an extra teaspoon **sugar** and 5-10 ml (1-2 tsp) **tamarind concentrate.**

◆ For SAMBAL KEMIRI, add **10 candlenuts** that have been dry roasted and ground.

NAM PRIK for cooked vegetables

125 g (4 oz) unripe fruit, such as green mango, gooseberries, tart plums or grapes
6 dried red chillies
a small piece of trassi (pp.154-5)
3 cloves garlic
1 onion
15 ml (1 tbsp) fish sauce (see *Simple Thai Fish Soup*, p.112)
1 tbsp soft brown sugar
lime juice

METHOD
Chop the unripe fruit. Remove the seeds from the chillies and chop. Wrap the trassi in foil and grill until it darkens, or cook in a preheated oven at 180°C, 350°F, gas 4 for a few minutes. Then, either crumble and pound, or process it with the other ingredients, adding lime juice to dilute and to taste. Store in a jar in the refrigerator for a few days.

Indian

MADRAS CURRY POWDER

A fragrant, fairly hot curry powder, which is used to flavour lamb and pork dishes.

2 dried red chillies
25 g (1 oz) coriander seeds
15 g (½ oz) cumin seeds
1 tsp mustard seeds
15 g (½ oz) black peppercorns
2 fresh curry leaves
½ tsp ground ginger
1 tsp ground turmeric

METHOD
Remove the seeds from the chillies. Dry roast the whole spices until they darken. Leave to cool, then grind to a powder. Dry roast the curry leaves in the pan for a few minutes, then grind and add them to the mixture with the ginger and turmeric, blending well. In an airtight jar, the powder will keep for 3-4 months.

Indian influenced

CHAR MASALA

Neighbouring Afghanistan uses this simpler blend of spices than India for flavouring rice dishes.

1 tbsp cinnamon
1 tbsp cloves
1 tbsp cumin seeds
1 tbsp black cardamom seeds

METHOD
Mix all the spices together. Stored in an airtight jar, the blend will keep for 3-4 months.

WEST INDIAN CURRY POWDER

Hindus who migrated to the West Indies in the 19th century introduced their spice blends to the islands, and curries are now found throughout the region.

25g (1oz) coriander seeds
1 tbsp of each of the following whole spices: aniseed, cumin, black mustard, fenugreek, black pepper
a piece of cinnamon
2 tbsp ground ginger
2 tbsp ground turmeric

METHOD
Dry roast all the whole spices for about 5 minutes. Cool, then grind and blend with the ginger and turmeric. In an airtight jar, the powder will keep for 3-4 months.

African & Middle Eastern
WAT SPICES

A wat is a traditional Ethiopian stew, spiced either with Berbere (pp.92-3) or this simpler blend of spices. The recipe below is taken from A *Safari of African Cooking* by Bill Odarty.

" 6 long peppers
  3 tablespoons black pepper
  3 tablespoons whole cloves
  1 long nutmeg
  a pinch of turmeric

Roast spices over a low flame. Pound them in order to break up big pieces. Place a pinch of turmeric on the grinding stone and grind until a yellow coating of turmeric is spread over the working surface. Grind all the other spices together on the yellow grinding stone. These spices are added to the wat towards the end of cooking.**"**

TUNISIAN FIVE SPICES

Called *qālat daqqa* in Arabic, this blend is used in vegetable dishes and with lamb.

2 tsp black peppercorns
2 tsp cloves
1 tsp grains of paradise
4 tsp grated nutmeg
1 tsp ground cinnamon

METHOD
Grind the peppercorns, cloves and grains of paradise together, then mix in the nutmeg and cinnamon. In an airtight jar, the blend will keep for 3-4 months.

DUKKA

This blend of spices with ground hazelnuts or roasted chick peas (available from Middle Eastern shops) comes from Egypt. Serve with bread: dip this in olive oil and then into the dukka.

125 g (4 oz) sesame seeds
75 g (3 oz) hazelnuts or roasted chick peas
50 g (2 oz) coriander seeds
25 g (1 oz) cumin seeds
1 tsp salt
¹/₂ tsp black peppercorns
1 tsp dried wild thyme or mint

METHOD
Dry roast the sesame seeds until lightly browned. Remove from the pan. Roast the hazelnuts for about 5 minutes and remove their skins (chick peas do not need roasting further), then roast the coriander and cumin seeds until they darken. When everything has cooled, combine all the ingredients and pound or process to a coarse powder. The mixture will keep for 3 months stored in an airtight jar in a cool place.

American
CRAB BOIL & FISH SEASONING

Crab boil is popular along the southeast coast of the United States, particularly in Louisiana. A similar blend, where the spices are ground, is used to spice fish.

1 tsp black peppercorns
1 tsp mustard seeds
1 tsp dill seeds
1 tsp coriander seeds
1 tsp cloves
1 tsp allspice berries
a small piece of dried ginger
3 dried bay leaves

METHOD
Tie the spices in a muslin bag and add to the water for boiling the crab.

4

Cooking with spices

Indispensable ingredients in all types of dishes – from soups, salads and casseroles to cakes, pickles and drinks – spices add and enhance flavours while also aiding digestion. The following pages provide more than 100 recipes based on different spices and spice mixtures from around the globe. All the spices used are described in the Spice Index (pp. 18–67); information about their preparation and storage is given on pp. 154–5. The amount of spicing in each recipe is a guide; adjust according to your own taste and preference.

Soups & starters

Pumpkin Soup

SERVES 4

This soup is cooked in the pumpkin, which makes a handsome presentation, although you can make it in a pan if you prefer. Salted dried shrimps, much used in Southeast Asian cooking, can be bought from Chinese shops. They give the soup a more robust flavour.

1 small pumpkin, about 20 cm (8 in) in diameter
salt
2 medium onions, chopped
3 tbsp long grain rice
½ tsp ground mace
½ tsp ground cinnamon
¼ tsp ground cumin
about 750 ml (1¼ pints) chicken stock
25 g (1 oz) salted dried shrimps (optional)
10 ml (2 tsp) lemon juice (optional)

1   Cut a lid from the top of the pumpkin and reserve. Discard the seeds and stringy tissue, then scoop out most of the pumpkin flesh, leaving a fairly thick coating round the sides and bottom. Chop the flesh.
2   Rub the inside of the pumpkin with a little salt and put it into a close-fitting ovenproof dish. Put in the pumpkin flesh, onions, rice and spices. Pour enough boiling chicken stock into the pumpkin to fill it by three-quarters, then close with its own lid. Cook at 160°C, 325°F, gas 3 for 2 hours.
3   If using dried shrimps, soak them in a little water to soften for 5–10 minutes. Pound the shrimps to a paste with the soaking water and lemon juice. Stir the paste into the soup for the last 20 minutes or so of the cooking time.
4   To serve, lift the pumpkin out into a warmed serving bowl. If it is too tricky to do this, bring the pumpkin to the table in the oven dish.

Mussel Soup with Saffron

SERVES 6

1 kg (2 lb) mussels
40 g (1½ oz) butter
1 onion, chopped
2 leeks, thinly sliced
1 carrot, diced
1 slice celeriac, about 125 g (4 oz), diced
900 ml (1½ pints) water
a few saffron threads, crushed
salt and pepper

1   Scrub the mussels, remove the beards and discard any that are broken or open. Just cover the bottom of a large pan with water, add the mussels, cover with a lid and cook over high heat, shaking the pan occasionally, until they open. Remove the mussels from their shells and set them aside. Discard any that have not opened. Strain the cooking liquid through muslin and reserve.
2   Melt the butter and sauté the onion, leeks and carrot for 5 minutes. Add the celeriac and cook gently for 10 minutes. Stir in the mussel liquor and water and simmer for 15 minutes.
3   Dissolve the saffron in a little hot water and stir into the soup. Season with salt and pepper.
4   Put the mussels into the soup just long enough to heat through, then serve.

Simple Thai Fish Soup

SERVES 4

Fish sauce, called *nam pla* in Thailand and *nuoc mam* in Vietnam, is the brown liquid drained off fish that has been fermented in brine. Its aroma is like that of ripe cheese, but the taste is more subdued. It is available from Oriental stores.

500 g (1 lb) firm white fish fillets
1.25 litres (2 pints) light fish stock
2 tsp ground galangal
2 stalks lemon grass, sliced and pounded
3 kaffir lime leaves
45 ml (3 tbsp) lime juice
1 tsp sambal oelek (pp. 74–5) or ground chilli
10 ml (2 tsp) fish sauce

Garnish
3–4 spring onions, chopped
1 tbsp chopped fresh coriander leaves
thin slices of lime

1   Cut the fish into small pieces. Bring the stock to the boil in a pan with the galangal, lemon grass and lime leaves. Simmer for 15 minutes, then strain.
2   Return the stock to the pan, add the fish, lime juice, sambal and fish sauce. Simmer gently for 4–5 minutes until the fish is cooked.
3   Remove the pan from the heat. Garnish with spring onion, coriander and lime slices, and serve.

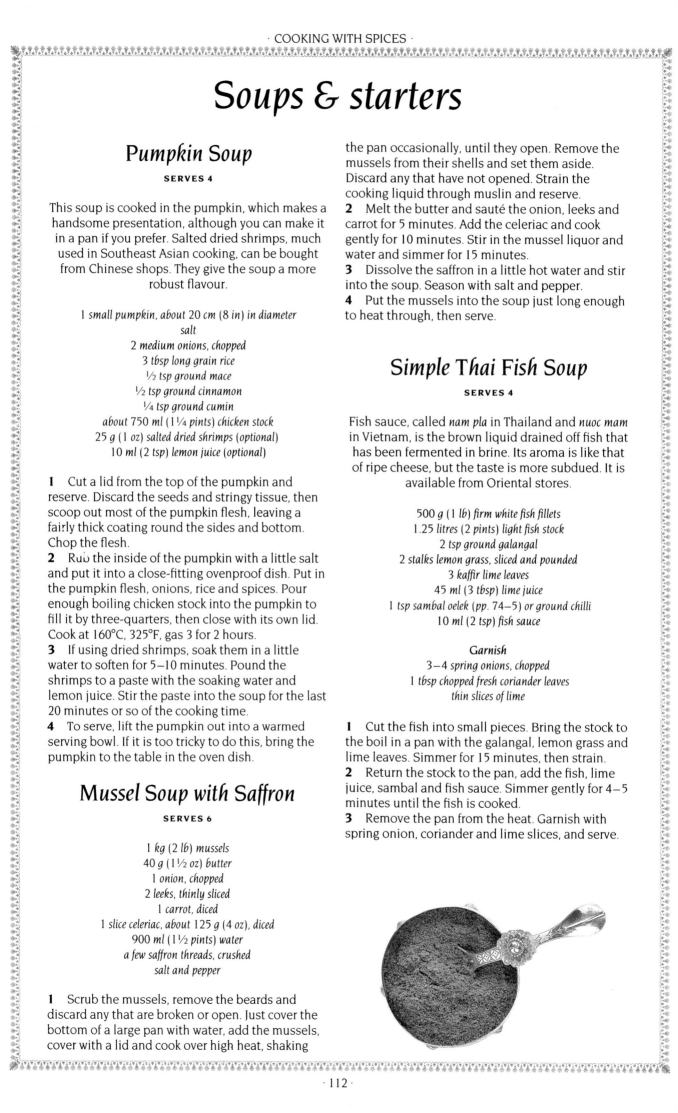

Chicken and Coconut Soup

SERVES 4

½ a small chicken
200 g (7 oz) creamed coconut dissolved in 1.25 litres (2 pints) hot water
1 tbsp ground galangal
3 stalks lemon grass, bruised and sliced
3 green chillies, seeded and sliced
3 spring onions, sliced
45 ml (3 tbsp) lime or lemon juice
30 ml (2 tbsp) fish sauce (see Simple Thai Fish Soup)
2 tbsp chopped fresh coriander leaves

1 Remove the skin from the chicken, and the bones if preferred. Cut the flesh into small chunks.
2 Bring the coconut milk to the boil in a large pan. Put in the chicken, galangal and lemon grass, and simmer for 15–20 minutes until the chicken is cooked. (Leave the pan open; if it is covered the steam in the pan will curdle the coconut milk.)
3 Stir in the remaining ingredients, and serve.

Spiced Lentil Soup

SERVES 6–8

½ tsp ground ginger
½ tsp ground black pepper
½ tsp ground turmeric
½ tsp ground fenugreek
¼ tsp ground cloves
2 tsp ground cumin
1 tsp ground cassia or cinnamon
grated rind of 1 lemon
60 ml (4 tbsp) olive oil
1 large onion, chopped
3 cloves garlic, crushed
175 g (6 oz) brown lentils
2 stalks celery, chopped
350 g (12 oz) tomatoes, chopped
1.5 litres (2½ pints) stock or water
salt
30–45 ml (2–3 tbsp) lemon juice
large bunch of fresh parsley or coriander, chopped
¼ tsp ground chilli (optional)

1 Mix all the spices, except the chilli, with the lemon rind.
2 Heat the oil in a large pan and gently cook the onion until soft. Add the spices and cook, stirring, for 2–3 minutes. Add the garlic and lentils and stir to coat the lentils with the oil and spices.
3 Add the celery and tomatoes and cook for a few minutes, then pour in the stock. Simmer steadily, covered, for about 1 hour until the lentils are soft. Add salt to taste and cook for a few minutes more.
4 Purée the soup, adding more stock or water if needed to achieve the required consistency. Stir in the lemon juice, the parsley or coriander and a sprinkling of ground chilli if liked.

Ceviche

SERVES 4

In this Mexican hors d'oeuvre, the fish is tenderized by marinating in lemon juice for several hours.

175 g (6 oz) salmon
175 g (6 oz) brill or turbot
175 g (6 oz) cod fillet
juice of 2–3 lemons
1–2 fresh green chillies, seeded and finely chopped
1 small mild onion, chopped
½ avocado, peeled, stoned and cubed
2 tomatoes, skinned, seeded and chopped
125 ml (4 fl oz) olive oil
handful of coriander leaves, chopped
salt and pepper

1 Remove any skin or bones from the fish and cut the flesh into small cubes. Put the cubes into a dish with the lemon juice, turn to coat all the fish and leave to marinate in the refrigerator for a minimum of 5 hours.
2 Drain the lemon juice from the fish and combine with the chopped vegetables, olive oil and coriander. Season with salt and pepper to taste and pour over the fish in a serving dish. Leave in the refrigerator until ready to serve.

Spiced Fish Mousse

SERVES 4–6

1 tsp ground anise
2 tsp ajowan
½ tsp chilli powder
2 cloves garlic, crushed with a little salt
500 g (1 lb) white fish fillets, cut in small pieces
175 g (6 oz) large cooked prawns, shelled weight
15 ml (1 tbsp) oil
1 onion, chopped
3 egg whites
handful of coriander leaves, chopped
salt
150 ml (¼ pint) double cream, whipped

1 Mix the anise, ajowan, chilli powder and garlic to a paste. Rub the fish with the paste and leave to marinate for 30 minutes.
2 Cut the prawns into two or three pieces. Heat the oil and sauté the onion until soft but not coloured. Remove from the heat and leave to cool.
3 Put the fish and onion in a food processor and chop finely.
4 Beat the egg whites until frothy and fold into the fish and onion mixture. Add the prawns and coriander, and a little salt. Fold in the cream.
5 Butter a 1 litre (1¾ pint) soufflé dish and pour in the mixture. Cook in a bain-marie (water bath) in a preheated oven at 140°C, 275°F, gas 1 for 45–50 minutes. Cool, then refrigerate for several hours before serving.

Indian Fruit Chat

SERVES 6

The fruit for this dish can vary according
to availability, but try to make sure that some of
it is tropical.

3 potatoes, boiled and diced
½ cucumber, peeled, seeded and cubed
2 ripe bananas, sliced
1 ripe papaya, cubed
1 ripe mango, cubed
1 apple, cubed
2 slices fresh pineapple, cubed
1 orange, in segments
2 tbsp chat masala (pp. 86–7)
juice of 1 lemon
lettuce leaves

1 Put all the vegetables and fruit into a bowl.
Sprinkle over the chat masala and lemon juice.
2 Arrange lettuce leaves on individual plates and
spoon over the fruit mixture.

Potted Shrimps or Prawns

SERVES 4

Small shrimps or prawns are best for potting, but
larger ones can be used, cut into pieces.

300 g (10 oz) cooked and peeled shrimps or prawns
175 g (6 oz) unsalted butter
large pinch of cayenne
½ tsp ground mace
black pepper
lemon juice

1 Divide the prepared shrimps or prawns among
four small ramekins.
2 Melt 125 g (4 oz) butter gently, remove from the
heat and pour off the clear liquid, leaving behind
the sediment. Stir in the cayenne and mace, some
freshly ground black pepper and a squeeze of
lemon juice.
3 Pour the spiced butter over the prawns and chill
the ramekins until the butter is firm. Then melt the
remaining butter and pour the clear liquid over the
prawns and butter to seal the pots. Chill again and
serve with toast and lemon wedges.

Shami Kebab

SERVES 4

500 g (1 lb) minced lamb
50 g (2 oz) yellow split peas
1 small onion, chopped
4 cloves garlic, chopped
1 tsp ground black cumin
1 tsp ground cinnamon
1 tsp chilli powder
1 tsp garam masala (pp. 84–5)
small bunch of coriander leaves, chopped
handful of cashew nuts, chopped
a little salt
2 eggs
30 ml (2 tbsp) lemon juice
oil for deep frying

1 Combine the minced lamb, split peas, onion,
garlic, spices, chopped coriander, cashew nuts and
a little salt.
2 Mince or process briefly to blend thoroughly.
Stir in the eggs and lemon juice.
3 Divide the mixture into eight. Wet your hands
and form each piece into a small flattened ball.
4 Heat the oil in a deep fryer and fry the kebabs in
two batches. Turn once and cook until brown on
both sides, about 3–4 minutes. Serve hot or at
room temperature, garnished with more chopped
coriander leaves.

Marinated Herring

SERVES 8

4 herrings, filleted
1 tsp salt
150 ml (¼ pint) milk
30 ml (2 tbsp) mustard
4 peppercorns
4 juniper berries
4 allspice berries
¼ tsp dill seeds
1 bouquet garni
1 onion, thinly sliced
450 ml (¾ pint) cider or wine vinegar
50 ml (2 fl oz) oil

1 Soak the herrings in salted milk for 3 hours.
Drain and pat dry.
2 Spread the fillets with mustard and roll up with
the skins on the outside. Fasten each one with a
wooden cocktail stick and put them in a large jar, or
a glass or china bowl.
3 Crush the peppercorns, juniper and allspice
lightly. Put them in a pan with the dill, bouquet
garni, onion and vinegar. Bring to the boil rapidly,
then simmer for 10 minutes. Allow the marinade to
cool slightly, then remove the bouquet garni.
4 Stir the oil into the marinade and pour over the
herrings. Cover and store in the refrigerator for 3–4
days before serving.

Fish dishes

Sea Bass Stuffed with Star Anise

SERVES 4

1 sea bass weighing 1.5 kg (3 lb)
1 tbsp chopped fresh ginger
30 ml (2 tbsp) Chinese rice wine or sherry
2 tsp Chinese five-spice powder (pp. 72–3)
4 star anise
4 spring onions, finely chopped
15 ml (1 tbsp) soy sauce
10 ml (2 tsp) Oriental sesame oil
salt

1 Cut two diagonal slits in each side of the bass.
2 Mix together the ginger, rice wine and five-spice powder, then rub the fish with the mixture. Leave to marinate for 1 hour.
3 Combine the star anise, spring onions, soy sauce and sesame oil with a little salt and use to stuff into the cavity of the fish. Wrap the fish in a large piece of oiled foil.
4 Bake in a preheated oven at 200°C, 400°F, gas 6 for 20–25 minutes.

Salmon with Ginger and Lime

SERVES 4

I keep a small jar of chopped fresh ginger "pickled" in sherry in the refrigerator. It is excellent for this dish, but chopped fresh ginger works well, too.

15 ml (1 tbsp) sesame oil
15 ml (1 tbsp) soy sauce
1 tbsp finely chopped fresh ginger
30 ml (2 tbsp) dry sherry
4 salmon steaks
salt
zest of 1 lime
2–3 spring onions or a few chives, chopped
1 lime, cut into wedges

1 Mix together the sesame oil, soy sauce, ginger and sherry, then rub the salmon steaks with the mixture. Leave to marinate for 30 minutes.
2 Heat a little water in a steamer, sprinkle the fish with salt and put it on a plate that fits in the steamer basket. Cover with foil. If you cannot fit a plate in the steamer, wrap the fish in foil.
3 Steam for about 12 minutes until the salmon is firm to the touch. Serve with its juices, sprinkled with the lime zest and chopped spring onion, and wedges of lime.

Fish Couscous

SERVES 6

Couscous with fish is popular along the Tunisian coast. Saffron, cumin and coriander are the usual spices; if you wish, use tabil (pp. 94–5) instead of the cumin and coriander. Grey mullet or bream would probably be used in Tunisia, but you could use any firm-fleshed fish. Reserve all the fish and vegetable trimmings so you can make a well-flavoured stock.

1.5 kg (3 lb) fish, cut into large slices
2 large onions, chopped
2 stalks celery, cut in chunks
3 carrots, cut in chunks
3 small turnips, quartered
3 courgettes, cut in chunks
125 g (4 oz) cabbage, shredded
125 g (4 oz) shelled peas
3 tomatoes, skinned and quartered
salt
pinch of cayenne
1.8 litres (3 pints) water
500 g (1 lb) couscous
45 ml (3 tbsp) oil
½ tsp saffron threads
1½ tsp tabil (pp. 94–5) or ground cumin and coriander
harissa (pp. 94–5) or paprika and cayenne, to taste

1 To make a fish stock, put the fish heads and vegetable trimmings, salt, cayenne and 1.2 litres (2 pints) water in a pan. Simmer for 20 minutes, then strain and reserve.
2 While the stock is cooking, prepare the couscous. Put the grain in a large bowl with 600 ml (1 pint) water. Stir well and leave for 10 minutes. Fluff up the grains between your fingers to get rid of any lumps. Sprinkle with 30 ml (2 tbsp) of the oil. The couscous is now ready to be steamed.
3 Heat the remaining oil in a large heavy pan and sauté the onions until golden. Add the celery, carrots, turnips and the stock made up to 1.8 litres (3 pints) with water. Stir in the saffron, tabil and salt to taste. Cover and simmer for 15 minutes. Add the remaining vegetables.
4 Put the couscous into a steamer, or in a colander lined with muslin that will fit on top of the pan, and simmer for 10 minutes. Check the liquid level and add more water if necessary, but keep it simmering steadily so that the steam penetrates the couscous. Add the fish to the stock and simmer until cooked, about 10–12 minutes.
5 Turn the couscous out into a large bowl, breaking up any lumps with a wooden fork. To make a hot-tasting sauce, take out a ladleful of stock and stir in harissa or paprika and cayenne to taste. Serve the stew on top of the couscous or separately.

Monkfish Parcels with Saffron

SERVES 4

750 g (1½ lb) monkfish, boned
salt and pepper
½–¾ tsp saffron threads
150 ml (¼ pint) dry white wine
150 ml (¼ pint) water
500 g (1 lb) large spinach leaves
butter

1 Cut the monkfish into cubes and season with salt and pepper.
2 Crush the saffron threads and soak in a little hot water for a few minutes. Heat the wine and water in a wide pan, add the saffron liquid and stir.
3 Put in the monkfish and simmer for 5–6 minutes. Drain carefully and reserve the liquid.
4 Select enough large spinach leaves to make three or four parcels per person. Wash the leaves, remove the stalks and blanch in boiling water for 2–3 minutes.
5 Arrange the leaves vein side up and put some pieces of monkfish at the stalk end. Wrap the parcels firmly, making sure the sides are tucked in. Put them into a buttered gratin dish with the end of the leaf underneath.
6 Strain the reserved cooking liquor over the parcels. Cover with foil and bake in a preheated oven at 180°C, 350°F, gas 4 for 15 minutes.

Monkfish Baked in Coconut Milk

SERVES 4

A very simple dish using the spicing of Southeast Asia.

1 kg (2 lb) monkfish
2 shallots, sliced
2 cloves garlic, sliced
piece of fresh ginger, peeled and sliced
¼ tsp ground chilli
½ tsp ground cumin
1 tsp ground coriander
¼ tsp ground galangal or piece of pounded root
salt
1 stalk lemon grass, crushed
25 g (1 oz) creamed coconut dissolved in 150 ml (¼ pint) hot water

1 Bone the fish and cut the flesh in four.
2 Combine the shallots, garlic and ginger and put half in the bottom of an ovenproof dish that is just large enough to take the fish in one layer.
3 Mix together the ground spices with salt to taste and rub on both sides of the fish. Place the fish in the dish, arrange the lemon grass between the pieces and put the rest of the vegetables on top. Pour over the coconut milk.
4 Cover and bake in a preheated oven at 180°C, 350°F, gas 4 for 30–40 minutes.

Grilled Tuna Steaks

SERVES 4

I keep a few small pots of Seville orange juice in the freezer to use in the summer; but if you do not have any, use half lemon and half orange juice. If you have a wire holder, the fish can be barbecued.

1 tsp ajowan
1 tsp green peppercorns
1 tsp chopped fresh tarragon
salt
2 large or 4 small tuna steaks
juice of 2 Seville oranges
olive oil

1 Crush the ajowan and peppercorns and mix with the tarragon and a little salt.
2 Rub the fish on both sides with the mixture and pour over the orange juice. Leave to marinate for at least 30 minutes.
3 Heat the grill, sprinkle a little oil over the fish and grill for about 10 minutes, turning once. Baste from time to time.

Prawn and Mango Curry

SERVES 4

500 g (1 lb) large prawns, shelled
salt
4 onions
3 cloves garlic, crushed
piece of fresh ginger, crushed
45 ml (3 tbsp) oil
6 green chillies, seeded and sliced
2 tbsp ground coriander
½ tsp ground turmeric or zedoary
1 tsp ground anise
1 tsp ground fenugreek
½ tsp mango powder
½ tsp mustard seeds
250 g (8 oz) creamed coconut dissolved in 450 ml (¾ pint) hot water
2 ripe mangoes, peeled and sliced

1 Rub the prawns with salt and set aside.
2 Slice two of the onions finely and chop the other two. Blend the crushed garlic and ginger to a paste with the chopped onion.
3 Heat the oil in a pan and fry the paste for 2–3 minutes, then add the sliced onion and the chillies and fry for a few minutes more. Stir in all the spices, then the coconut milk. Simmer for 8–10 minutes, uncovered, stirring to make sure it does not stick.
4 Put in the prawns and mango and simmer, covered, for 6–7 minutes until the prawns are cooked through. Do not overcook or they will become tough. Serve with rice.

Prawn and mango curry with ginger, fenugreek, anise, mango powder, turmeric, mustard seeds and coriander.

Spiced Crab with Green Beans

SERVES 4

250 g (8 oz) small green beans
90 ml (6 tbsp) dry sherry
30 ml (2 tbsp) sesame oil
15 ml (1 tbsp) soy sauce
2.5 ml (½ tsp) chilli sauce
½ tsp ground fagara
15 ml (1 tbsp) oil
zest of ½ a lemon
2 cloves garlic, chopped
350 g (12 oz) white crab meat, shredded
4 spring onions, finely sliced

1   Cook the green beans in a pan of boiling water until just tender.
2   Mix together the sherry, sesame oil, soy sauce, chilli sauce and fagara, then set aside.
3   Heat the oil in a pan and sauté the lemon rind and garlic briefly. Stir in the crab meat and cook for 1–2 minutes.
4   Pour over the sauce, toss to coat the crab and heat through. Turn out into the centre of a warmed serving dish, sprinkle the spring onion over the top and surround with the beans.

Scallops and Leeks with Star Anise

SERVES 4

8 scallops
25 g (1 oz) butter
2 shallots, finely chopped
350 g (12 oz) small leeks, finely chopped
½ glass dry white wine
2 star anise
15 ml (1 tbsp) lemon juice
`salt and white pepper
30 ml (2 tbsp) double cream

1   Detach the coral from the scallops and cut the white flesh in half horizontally.
2   Heat the butter in a heavy pan and stew the shallots gently for a few minutes. Add the leeks, half of the wine and the star anise. Season with salt and pepper, cover and simmer slowly for 15 minutes. Remove from the heat.
3   Put the remaining wine in a small pan with the lemon juice. Add the scallops, bring to the boil and simmer for about one minute – until the scallops are opaque. Lift them out carefully.
4   Strain the leeks and add any cooking liquor and the star anise to the scallop pan. Arrange the leeks on four individual plates, top with the scallops and keep warm.
5   Reduce the juices to 45–60 ml (3–4 tbsp), then stir in the cream. Check the seasoning and spoon over the scallops and leeks.

Baked Cod with Mustard

SERVES 4

4 cod steaks
salt and white pepper
30 ml (2 tbsp) Dijon mustard
40 g (1½ oz) butter
350 g (12 oz) leeks, finely sliced
2 heads chicory, finely sliced
30–45 ml (2–3 tbsp) white wine or water

1   Season the fish with salt and pepper. Spread the mustard on both sides of the fish.
2   Melt the butter in a pan and cook the leeks and chicory until just wilted. Drain and transfer half to a buttered ovenproof dish.
3   Lay the cod steaks on the bed of vegetables and top each one with some of the remaining leeks and chicory. Spoon over the wine.
4   Cover and bake in a preheated oven at 200°C, 400°F, gas 6 for 20–30 minutes.

Oriental Seafood Salad

SERVES 6–8

The combination of seafood here is just a suggestion; quantities and types may be varied according to what is available.

350 g (12 oz) baby squid
500 g (1 lb) baby octopus
450 ml (¾ pint) fish stock
500 g (1 lb) uncooked medium prawns
500g (1 lb) spinach, shredded
1 cucumber
½ small melon
2 red peppers
2 papayas
handful of pine nuts

Dressing
juice of 1½ lemons
2 tbsp soft brown sugar
10 ml (2 tsp) chilli sauce
5–6 spring onions, finely chopped
piece of fresh ginger, peeled and finely chopped
30 ml (2 tbsp) fish sauce (see Simple Thai Fish Soup, p.112)
small bunch of coriander leaves, chopped
90 ml (6 tbsp) sunflower oil
salt

1   Clean the squid and cut into rings; the octopus can be cooked whole. Poach them in fish stock until tender – about 12 minutes for the squid and 20 minutes for the octopus. Drain and put aside.
2   Cook the prawns in a large pan of boiling salted water for 2–3 minutes until pink on the outside and white inside. Drain and plunge into iced water to cool them quickly. Drain and shell them.
3   Blanch the spinach for 1 minute, then drain and squeeze out all the moisture.

4 Cut the cucumber and melon into small cubes; cut the peppers and papaya to the same size. Toast the pine nuts in a dry frying pan until golden.
5 Combine the remaining ingredients to make a dressing, but taste before adding salt.
6 Spread the spinach on a large platter. Arrange the seafood, vegetables, fruit and nuts over it, then spoon over the dressing and serve.

Crab with Avocado and Ginger

SERVES 2

A light salad for two, or serve as a first course for four.

250 g (8 oz) white crab meat, shredded
2 tbsp Japanese pickled ginger, drained
zest of ½ a lemon
juice of ½–1 lemon
1 avocado, peeled, halved and stoned
a few rocket leaves
olive oil
sansho (p. 61), to serve

1 Marinate the crab with the pickled ginger, the zest and most of the lemon juice for 30 minutes.
2 Slice the avocado and brush with the remaining lemon juice to prevent it discolouring.
3 Place a few rocket leaves on four plates. Arrange avocado slices on one side of each plate and some of the crab and ginger on the other. Pour a little olive oil over everything and serve with sansho.

Warm Mussel Salad

SERVES 4—6

1.5 kg (3 lb) mussels, cleaned (p. 112)
150 ml (¼ pint) dry white wine
500 g (1 lb) Pink Fir or other waxy potatoes
1 cucumber, cubed
salt
30 ml (2 tbsp) olive oil
4 shallots, chopped
1 tsp ground aniseed
5 stalks celery, sliced
90 ml (6 tbsp) cream

1 Place the mussels in a large pan with the white wine. Cover and cook, shaking the pan from time to time, until the mussels have opened. Drain, reserve the liquor and discard the mussel shells and any mussels that have not opened.
2 Boil the potatoes until tender and drain. Slice them thickly.
3 Sprinkle the cucumber with salt and leave to drain for 30 minutes.
4 Heat the oil and sauté the shallots for a few minutes, then add the aniseed and stir for 2–3 minutes. Add the celery, potatoes and cucumber to the pan.
5 Strain the mussel liquor through muslin, add about 150 ml (¼ pint) to the pan and simmer for 5 minutes. Taste for seasoning.
6 Add the mussels and cream, stir carefully to blend, and serve.

Meat dishes

Lamb with Pomegranate Juice

SERVES 4—6

45 ml (3 tbsp) sunflower oil
3 cardamoms, crushed
3 cloves
1 tsp fenugreek seeds
1 kg (2 lb) lean lamb, cubed
1 large onion, sliced
2 cloves garlic, finely chopped
small piece of fresh ginger, peeled and finely chopped
juice of 2 pomegranates, about 300 ml (½ pint),
or 45 ml (3 tbsp) pomegranate syrup diluted with water
½ tsp ground black cumin
½ tsp ground cinnamon
½ tsp ground mace
salt
75 ml (5 tbsp) natural yogurt
chopped mint leaves

1 Heat the oil in a heavy pan and fry the whole spices briefly to bring out their flavour, shaking and stirring them so they do not burn.

2 Discard the spices, add the meat, tossing and stirring to brown it on all sides. Continue cooking until the meat re-absorbs its juices.
3 Add the onion, garlic and ginger and cook until the onion colours. Stir in the pomegranate juice, a little at a time, waiting until each addition is absorbed by the meat before adding more. There should be very little liquid left, except the oil.
4 Stir in the ground spices and salt to taste, then fry briefly. Add the yogurt.
5 Cover the pan tightly, put it on a heat diffuser and cook very slowly for 30–40 minutes until the lamb is tender. Check once or twice that the meat is not sticking, and add a little more yogurt or water if necessary. Garnish with chopped mint leaves and serve with rice.

Lamb Kofta

SERVES 4

These spicy minced meat kebabs are popular throughout the Middle East.

500 g (1 lb) lean lamb, minced twice
1 medium onion, finely chopped
handful of chopped fresh parsley
1 tsp ground allspice
¼ tsp ground fenugreek
pinch of ground red pepper
salt
oil for brushing
lemon wedges
ground sumac

1   Put the meat, onion, parsley, allspice, fenugreek, pepper and salt to taste into a large bowl and mix thoroughly.
2   Divide into four and, wetting your hands if necessary, form each piece into a sausage shape around a broad, flat skewer.
3   Brush each one lightly with oil and grill, preferably over charcoal, for 10–15 minutes, turning the skewers from time to time.
4   Serve the kofta with lemon wedges and a bowl of ground sumac to be sprinkled on them, if liked.

Lamb with Chick Peas and Lentils

SERVES 4

A version of a Turkish stew that makes an excellent winter dish.

4 large lamb chops
125 g (4 oz) chick peas, soaked overnight
125 g (4 oz) brown lentils, washed
1.8 litres (3 pints) water
50 g (2 oz) butter
2 large onions, chopped
30 ml (2 tbsp) tomato purée
1 tsp Turkish red pepper, or ½ tsp paprika and ½ tsp cayenne
1 tbsp coriander seeds, ground
salt and pepper
2 large potatoes, thickly sliced

1   Trim any excess fat from the meat and put the chops into a large pan with the chick peas, lentils and water. Bring slowly to the boil, then skim.
2   Meanwhile, melt the butter in a pan and sauté the onions until softened. Stir in the tomato purée, spices and seasoning. Remove from the heat and add to the meat, together with the potatoes.
3   Cover and simmer over low heat for 1½–2 hours until the chick peas are cooked and the stew is thick and rich. Check that there is enough liquid towards the end of the cooking time – if not, add a little more hot water before serving.

Lamb Mrouziya

SERVES 6

In the past, this Moroccan tagine served as a way of preserving the meat in a culture where freezing and refrigeration were not common.

a few saffron stamens
2 tsp ras el hanout (pp. 96–7)
1 tsp ground black pepper
1 tsp ground cinnamon
salt
1.5 kg (3 lb) middle neck of lamb, with bone
250 g (8 oz) raisins
175 g (6 oz) blanched almonds
3 onions, finely chopped
125 g (4 oz) butter
150 ml (¼ pint) water
175 g (6 oz) thick honey

1   Powder the saffron and mix with the other spices and salt to taste. Rub the meat with most of the mixture and sprinkle the rest on the raisins.
2   Put the meat into a heavy pan with the almonds, onions, and butter. Add the water, bring to the boil, then simmer for 1–1½ hours until the meat is almost tender, adding more water as necessary to prevent the meat from burning.
3   Stir in the raisins and honey and simmer gently for a further 30 minutes, uncovered, until most of the liquid has evaporated and a thick, rich sauce has formed. Lift the lamb on to a warmed serving dish and cover with the sauce.

Thai Beef Curry

SERVES 6

45 ml (3 tbsp) oil
750 g (1½ lb) braising or stewing beef, cubed
4 onions, quartered
500 g (1 lb) potatoes, cubed same size as meat
30 ml (2 tbsp) red curry paste (pp. 78–9)
30 ml (2 tbsp) fish sauce (see Simple Thai Fish Soup, p. 112)
1 ball tamarind soaked in 45 ml (3 tbsp) hot water
1 tbsp sugar
350 g (12 oz) creamed coconut dissolved in 900 ml (1½ pints) hot water
3 curry leaves
6 cardamoms, crushed

1   Heat the oil and brown the beef on all sides. Remove the beef and cook the onions and potatoes in the oil for a few minutes, then remove them.
2   Fry the curry paste, add the fish sauce, tamarind water, sugar and coconut milk, and bring to the boil.
3   Reduce the heat, return the meat and vegetables to the pan with the curry leaves and cardamom. Cover and simmer for about 2 hours. Check from time to time to make sure that it is not sticking and add a little water if necessary.

Sichuan Noodles with Beef

SERVES 6

350 g (12 oz) lean sirloin steak
60 ml (4 tbsp) soy sauce
45 ml (3 tbsp) rice vinegar
1 tsp finely chopped garlic
1 tsp finely chopped fresh ginger
1 tsp sugar
2–3 chillies, seeded and sliced
4 spring onions, finely chopped
small handful of coriander leaves, finely chopped
60 ml (4 tbsp) groundnut oil
350 g (12 oz) dried egg noodles
1 tbsp toasted sesame seeds
6 whole spring onions

1   Cut the steak across the grain into thin strips.
2   Make a marinade with the soy sauce, rice vinegar, garlic, ginger, sugar, chillies, chopped spring onions, coriander and 30 ml (2 tbsp) of the oil. Marinate the beef for 30 minutes.
3   Heat the remaining oil in a wok or heavy frying pan. Drain the meat from the marinade and sauté for 2 minutes.
4   Meanwhile, cook the noodles in a pan of boiling salted water for 5–7 minutes until *al dente*. Drain and place in a large, warmed serving dish. Pour over the remaining beef marinade.
5   Make a slight indentation in the centre of the noodles and spoon in the beef. Sprinkle with the sesame seeds and garnish the dish with the whole spring onions.

Hungarian Veal Paprikash

SERVES 4

25 g (1 oz) lard or butter
1 large onion, chopped
1 kg (2 lb) lean veal, cubed
1 large tomato, skinned and chopped
1–1½ tsp paprika
salt
1 green pepper, sliced
300 ml (½ pint) sour cream
1 tbsp flour

1   Melt the lard in a heavy pan and fry the onion until transparent. Turn the heat as low as possible and add the veal, tomato, paprika and salt to taste.
2   Cover and simmer very gently, stirring occasionally and adding a few tablespoons of water to prevent the meat sticking, if necessary.
3   After 20 minutes or so, add the green pepper. Continue to cook for a further 20 minutes until the veal is almost done. Cook until any remaining liquid evaporates.
4   Blend the sour cream with the flour, then stir into the pan. Cover again and simmer very slowly until the meat is tender. Serve with little egg dumplings or noodles.

Spiced Veal Boulangère

SERVES 6—8

4 cloves garlic
salt and pepper
½ tsp ground mace
¼ tsp ground cardamom
¾ tsp ground cinnamon
2 kg (4 lb) loin of veal, boned and rolled
olive oil
1 kg (2 lb) potatoes, sliced
300 ml (½ pint) water

1   Crush 2 cloves of garlic with a little salt and mix with half of the spices and a few grindings of pepper.
2   Pierce the meat here and there with the point of a sharp knife and insert the garlic and spice mixture. Rub the surface of the meat with oil and the rest of the spices. Finely slice the remaining 2 cloves of garlic.
3   Place the meat in a roasting tin. Brown in a preheated oven at 230°C, 450°F, gas 8 for 10 minutes. Take the tin from the oven and distribute the potatoes under and around the meat, seasoning layers with salt, pepper and slivers of garlic. Add the water.
4   Cover the tin with foil, return to the oven and cook at 160°C, 325°F, gas 3 for 1½ hours. Remove the foil and cook for a further 15 minutes. Rest the meat for 10 minutes in a warm place before carving.

Pork with Fennel

SERVES 6

¾ tsp fennel seeds, ground
½ tsp black peppercorns, crushed
salt
1 kg (2 lb) loin of pork, bones and skin removed, and rolled
1 onion, sliced
1 carrot, sliced
150 ml (¼ pint) water
1 tsp cornflour
150 ml (¼ pint) sour cream

1   Mix together the fennel and pepper with salt to taste. Rub the meat all over with the seasoning.
2   Put the onion and carrot in a small roasting tin. Lay the meat on the vegetables and pour the water around the pork.
3   Roast in a preheated oven at 200°C, 400°F, gas 6 for about 1 hour 20 minutes, basting the meat every 10 minutes or so. Add a little more water to the meat if necessary.
4   When the pork is cooked, remove it and leave to stand in a warm place for 10 minutes or so before starting to carve it.
5   To make the sauce, scrape the vegetables and other sediment loose in the pan. Stir the cornflour into the sour cream and whisk into the pan juices. Heat through, taste for seasoning and strain into a sauce boat.

Pork Satay

SERVES 6—8

A popular dish with the Chinese of Southeast Asia.

1 onion, finely chopped
2 cloves garlic, crushed
1 tbsp Chinese five-spice powder (pp. 72-3)
small piece of fresh ginger, crushed
60 ml (4 tbsp) light soy sauce
15 ml (1 tbsp) honey
75–90 ml (5–6 tbsp) sunflower oil
1 kg (2 lb) pork fillet, cubed
2 stalks lemon grass, finely sliced

1   Blend together all the ingredients, except the
pork and lemon grass, to make a smooth marinade.
2   Put the pork cubes and lemon grass in a bowl,
coat thoroughly with the marinade and leave for at
least 2 hours.
3   Thread the meat on to skewers and grill for
15–20 minutes until cooked. Serve with peanut
sauce (p. 142) or Indonesian soy relish (p. 142).

Chicken Satay

SERVES 6—8

Serve this popular dish with peanut sauce (p. 142).

1 kg (2 lb) chicken breast
small piece of fresh ginger, crushed
3 cloves garlic, crushed
1 tbsp ground coriander
½ tsp ground galangal
15 ml (1 tbsp) oil
50 g (2 oz) creamed coconut dissolved in 150 ml (¼ pint)
hot water

1   Remove the skin from the chicken and cut the
flesh into strips.
2   Combine the remaining ingredients in a
blender or food processor to make a smooth
marinade. Use to coat the chicken thoroughly.
Leave to marinate for at least 2 hours.
3   Thread the pieces of meat on to small wooden
skewers and grill for 5–6 minutes, turning as
necessary to cook all sides.

Afelia

SERVES 4

750 g (1½ lb) pork fillet
50 g (2 oz) olive oil
salt and pepper
150 ml (¼ pint) red wine
1 tbsp coriander seeds, crushed

1   Remove any fat from the pork and cut the flesh
into cubes. Heat the oil in a heavy pan and brown
the meat on all sides. Season with salt and pepper.
2   Pour over the wine, bring to the boil, then cover
and simmer gently for 20 minutes.
3   Stir in the coriander, cover, and simmer for
another 20–25 minutes until the meat is tender
and most of the liquid absorbed. Check the pan
from time to time and add more wine, if necessary.

Cold Spiced Chicken

SERVES 6

45 ml (3 tbsp) natural yogurt
½ tsp garam masala (pp. 84–5)
½ tsp ground turmeric
salt
6 chicken breasts, skinned
600 ml (1 pint) chicken stock
4 green cardamoms
1 curry leaf or bay leaf

Sauce
25 g (1 oz) butter
1 tbsp gram flour
½ tbsp plain flour
½ tsp garam masala
½ tsp ground turmeric
about 450 ml (¾ pint) reserved chicken stock
½ tsp ground mace
¼ tsp ground cardamom
60 ml (4 tbsp) double cream or thick yogurt

1   Blend together the yogurt, garam masala,
turmeric and salt to taste. Rub the chicken breasts
with the mixture and marinate for 1 hour.
2   Heat the stock with the cardamoms and curry
leaf. Put in the chicken breasts and simmer for
15–20 minutes or until tender.
3   Lift out the chicken and transfer to a serving
dish. Strain and reserve the stock. Leave to cool
while making the sauce.
4   Melt the butter in a pan and stir in the flours
until smooth. Add the garam masala, turmeric and
a little salt, then whisk in the reserved stock. Bring
to the boil and simmer for 15 minutes, stirring
occasionally. Stir in the mace, cardamom and
cream or yogurt. Spoon over the chicken and chill
before serving.

*Cold spiced chicken with turmeric, mace, cardamoms, curry
leaves and garam masala.*

Chicken with Noodles

SERVES 4

A simple and comforting Japanese dish. Dashi granules or powder, requiring only the addition of water to make the stock, can be bought from Japanese shops. A good chicken stock can be used as a substitute. Mirin – very sweet rice wine used only for cooking – can, at a pinch, be replaced by sweet sherry and a spoonful of sugar.

350 g (12 oz) udon or other wheat noodles
350 g (12 oz) chicken, skinned and boned
6 spring onions
750 ml (1¼ pints) dashi
60 ml (4 tbsp) soy sauce
30 ml (2 tbsp) mirin
shichimi (pp. 70–1), to serve

1   Boil the noodles in a pan until tender. Drain and rinse under cold running water.
2   Cut the chicken into small pieces. Cut the spring onions, including the green part, into 1.5 cm (½ in) lengths.
3   Combine the dashi, soy sauce and mirin in a pan and bring to the boil. Add the chicken and simmer for 5–6 minutes or until tender. Stir in the spring onions and simmer for 1 minute.
4   Reheat the noodles by pouring boiling water over them. Divide between four large warmed bowls. Ladle over the stock and arrange the chicken and onions on top. Serve with shichimi.

Chicken Braised with Coriander

SERVES 4

1 large onion, roughly chopped
4 cloves garlic
6 candlenuts
1 tbsp ground coriander
5 ml (1 tsp) tamarind concentrate
½ tsp ground turmeric
¼ tsp ground galangal
3–4 hot chillies, seeded if preferred
1 tsp sugar
salt
1 medium chicken, cut into pieces
250 g (8 oz) creamed coconut dissolved in 450 ml (¾ pint)
hot water
2 kaffir lime leaves or 1 bay leaf
piece of lemon grass or ¼ tsp ground

1   Pound together or process the onion, garlic, candlenuts, coriander, tamarind, turmeric, galangal, chillies and sugar with salt to taste.
2   Rub the chicken with the paste and leave for about 1 hour.
3   Transfer the chicken to a pan. Add the coconut milk, lime leaves and lemon grass. Braise gently in an open pan for about 45 minutes until the sauce thickens and the oil starts to glisten on the surface.

4   The chicken can be served straight away or it can be lifted from the pan and grilled, basting occasionally with oil, until lightly browned. Serve the sauce separately.

VARIATIONS

◆   In Indonesia, the pieces of chicken are often deep fried before serving.
◆   Use yogurt, stabilized with 1 tbsp cornflour blended with a little milk, instead of coconut milk.

Chicken and Groundnut Stew

SERVES 4—6

Stews and soups based on groundnuts (peanuts) are common throughout West Africa. This is a simple version using peanut butter, though you could grind plain peanuts instead. The vegetables can be varied according to what is available, but for an authentic taste keep the okra, aubergine and cabbage. Sweet potato is a good alternative to ordinary potato.

60 ml (4 tbsp) groundnut oil
1 chicken, cut in pieces
1 large onion, chopped
2 tomatoes, peeled and chopped
15 ml (1 tbsp) tomato purée
600 ml (1 pint) boiling water
175 g (6 oz) peanut butter
salt
1 tsp grains of paradise or black peppercorns, crushed
2 carrots, sliced
1 small aubergine, cubed
2 potatoes, peeled and cubed
½ small cabbage, sliced
175 g (6 oz) okra

1   Heat the oil in a large pan and brown the chicken. Remove and set aside. Add the onion and cook for a few minutes, then stir in the tomatoes and tomato purée. Return the chicken to the pan.
2   Pour on a little of the water and use the rest to thin the peanut butter. Add this to the pan and season with salt and grains of paradise. Stir well, cover, reduce the heat and simmer gently for 20 minutes, checking occasionally to see that the sauce is not sticking – it should be thick, but if necessary add a little more water.
3   Add the carrots and aubergine and continue cooking for 10 minutes. Stir in the potatoes and cabbage gently and cook for a further 15 minutes, or until the chicken and vegetables are tender. Put in the okra, simmer for 5 minutes more, then serve.

Venison with Sour Cherry Sauce

SERVES 6

90 ml (6 tbsp) olive oil
30 ml (2 tbsp) lemon juice
1 tbsp juniper berries, crushed
1 tsp salt
1 bay leaf, crumbled
2 kg (4 lb) saddle of venison
pork fat, to cover
1 onion, sliced
125 ml (4 fl oz) red wine
250 g (8 oz) morello cherries, stoned
30–45 ml (2–3 tbsp) redcurrant jelly
¼ tsp ground allspice
pinch of ground cinnamon
stock or water, if necessary

1 Combine 45 ml (3 tbsp) of the oil with the lemon juice, juniper, salt and bay leaf and rub over the venison. Leave to marinate for 2–3 hours.
2 Spread the pork fat over the meat. Put the sliced onion in a roasting tin and arrange the meat on top. Add the remaining oil and the wine.
3 Roast in a preheated oven at 180°C, 350°F, gas 4 for about 1¼ hours, basting frequently. Check to see if the meat is done – it should still be slightly rare and pink inside. Remove and leave to stand in a warm place while preparing the sauce.
4 Scrape loose any sediment stuck to the bottom of the roasting tin, stir briskly over medium heat and remove any excess fat. Strain the juices into a pan; there should be at least 150 ml (¼ pint) – if necessary add a little stock or water. Put in the cherries, jelly and spices and heat gently. Carve the venison, spoon over the sauce and serve.

Noisettes of Venison with Green Peppercorns

SERVES 4

50 g (2 oz) butter
8 noisettes of venison
4 shallots, finely chopped
30 ml (2 tbsp) brandy or armagnac
15 ml (1 tbsp) French mustard
250 ml (8 fl oz) stock
1 tbsp green peppercorns
150 ml (¼ pint) crème fraîche or double cream
salt

1 Melt the butter in a frying pan and sauté the venison 3–4 minutes on each side until lightly browned. Remove to a serving dish and keep warm.
2 Add the shallots to the pan and cook for 3–4 minutes. Heat the brandy in a small pan or ladle, then ignite and pour over the shallots.
3 Stir in the mustard, add the stock and bring to the boil. Boil rapidly to reduce by half, then add the peppercorns, cream and salt to taste. Heat through, spoon over the noisettes and serve.

Pheasant Chilindrón

SERVES 4

This dish from the province of Aragon in Spain can also be made with chicken or pork or lamb chops. The name *chilindrón* refers to the red peppers used in the dish. Use Spanish serrano ham if possible.

2 small pheasants, cut in half
salt
60 ml (4 tbsp) olive oil
1 clove garlic, chopped
1 onion, chopped
75 g (3 oz) smoked ham, diced
a few saffron threads, toasted briefly
2 tsp paprika
2 red peppers, cut in strips
2 large tomatoes, skinned and chopped
1 red chilli (optional)

1 Season the pheasants with salt. Heat the oil in a pan and sauté the pheasants until browned. Lift out and sauté the garlic and onion until the onion is softened.
2 Add the ham, saffron, paprika, red peppers and tomatoes. Cover and cook for 10 minutes, then return the pheasant halves to the pan. Add more salt, if necessary, and the chilli if using. Cover and simmer for 40 minutes.
3 Uncover and cook for another 20 minutes until the pheasant is tender and the sauce quite thick.

Rabbit with Mustard Sauce

SERVES 6

75 g (3 oz) butter
15 ml (1 tbsp) oil
2 rabbits, cut into pieces
sprig of fresh thyme or 1 tsp dried thyme
1 bay leaf
salt and pepper
4 shallots, finely chopped
150 ml (¼ pint) dry white wine
30 ml (2 tbsp) Dijon mustard
juice of ½ a lemon
125 ml (4 fl oz) double cream
chopped fresh parsley, to garnish

1 Heat 25 g (1 oz) of the butter and the oil in a flameproof casserole and sauté the rabbit until well browned. Season with the thyme, bay leaf and salt and pepper. Cover tightly.
2 Cook in a preheated oven at 160°C, 325°F, gas 3 for 50 minutes.
3 Heat the remaining butter in a pan and sauté the shallots. Moisten with the wine and reduce by half. Stir in the mustard, lemon juice and cream, then heat through.
4 Put the rabbit pieces on a warmed serving dish, pour over the sauce, and sprinkle with parsley.

Rabbit in Sour Cream with Caraway

SERVES 4

1 rabbit, jointed
65 g (2½ oz) butter
2 onions, chopped
2 carrots, diced
1 parsnip, diced
2 tbsp flour
150 ml (¼ pint) stock or water
300 ml (½ pint) sour cream
½ tsp ground caraway
salt and pepper

Marinade
1 onion, chopped
1 carrot, chopped
1 stalk celery, chopped
3 cloves garlic, crushed
2 bay leaves
sprig of thyme
1 tsp allspice berries, crushed
1 tsp black peppercorns, crushed
150 ml (¼ pint) cider vinegar
300 ml (½ pint) water

1   For the marinade, put the onion, carrot, celery, garlic, bay leaves, thyme, allspice, peppercorns, vinegar and water in a pan and bring to the boil. Allow to cool.
2   Pour the marinade over the rabbit. Leave to marinate for up to 24 hours.
3   Melt 40 g (1½ oz) of the butter in a heavy flameproof casserole and sauté the onions, carrots and parsnip for 5 minutes. Add the drained rabbit and brown gently.
4   Melt the remaining butter in a pan and stir in the flour until smooth. Add the stock gradually, stirring until well blended and bring to the boil. Stir in the sour cream, caraway and seasonings.
5   Pour the sauce over the rabbit, stirring well to amalgamate the pan juices. Cover and simmer for 40–50 minutes. Serve with noodles or potatoes.

Rabbit with Fennel and Garlic

SERVES 4

1 rabbit, cut into serving pieces
300 ml (½ pint) white wine
45 ml (3 tbsp) olive oil
2 tsp fennel seeds
salt
1 small onion, finely chopped
salt and pepper
175 g (6 oz) young runner beans, cut into pieces
175 g (6 oz) broad beans
1 head garlic
150 ml (¼ pint) cream and water, mixed

1   Marinate the rabbit in the wine with 30 ml (2 tbsp) of the oil, the fennel seeds and a little salt for 2–3 hours. Drain the meat and pat dry, reserving the marinade.
2   Heat the remaining oil and brown the rabbit. Add the onion, and sauté until transparent.
3   Stir in the marinade, bring to the boil and season with salt and pepper. Simmer gently for about 20 minutes.
4   Cook the runner beans and broad beans briefly in boiling water. Drain and add to the rabbit and cook for another 20 minutes.
5   Separate the garlic into cloves and blanch in boiling water for 3–4 minutes. Drain, cool and peel. Simmer the garlic in the cream and water for 15 minutes, then crush to a purée.
6   Check that the rabbit is tender, then stir in the purée. Serve with new potatoes.

Baked Liver

SERVES 4

A rich and delicate dish that can also be made with lamb's liver.

500 g (1 lb) calf's liver
1 tsp trassi (pp. 154–5)
25 g (1 oz) creamed coconut dissolved in 60 ml (4 tbsp) hot water
2 tsp ground coriander
15 ml (1 tbsp) lemon juice
a few kaffir lime leaves, crushed, or ¼ tsp ground lemon grass

1   Dice the liver or cut it into thin strips.
2   Wrap the trassi in a piece of foil and heat through in a dry pan or medium oven (180°C, 350°F, gas 4) for a few minutes, then crumble it.
3   Combine the coconut milk, coriander, lemon juice, trassi and lime leaves to make a thick marinade. Coat the liver in the marinade in an ovenproof dish and leave for at least 1 hour.
4   Cook in a preheated oven at 180°C, 350°F, gas 4 for 20 minutes for thin strips of liver, and 25–30 minutes for larger pieces. The liver will have a very good texture and be pale pink in the middle.

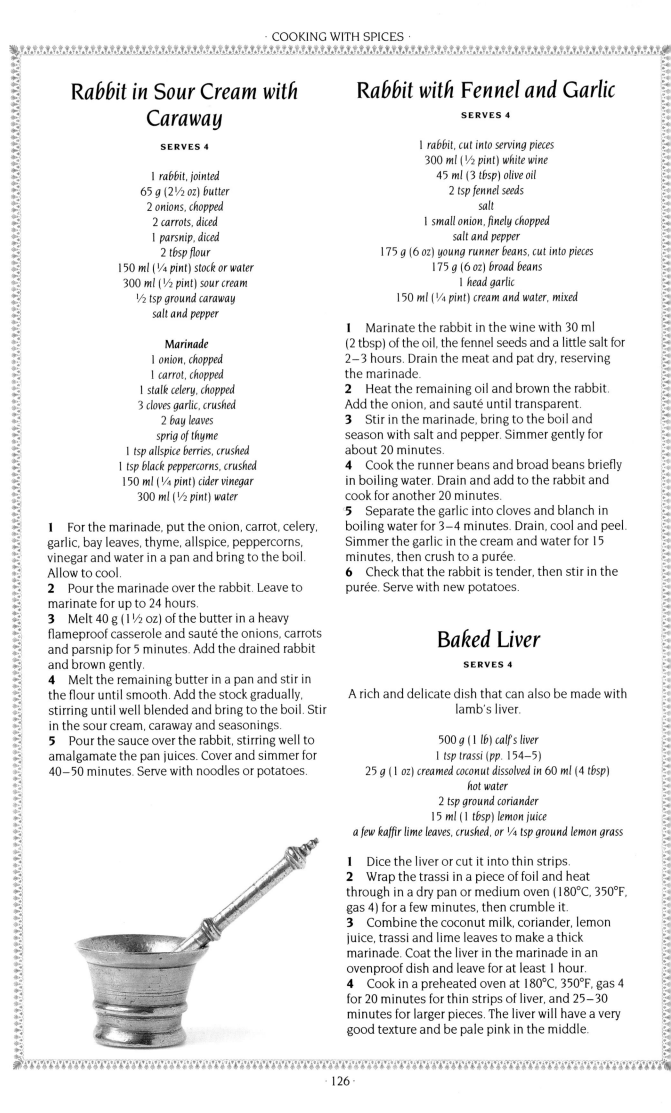

Vegetable & grain dishes

Stir-fried Noodles with Mange-touts and Prawns

SERVES 6

500 g (1 lb) Chinese flat noodles
salt
2–3 cloves garlic
2 stalks lemon grass
30 ml (2 tbsp) groundnut oil
small piece of fresh ginger, peeled and finely chopped
350 g (12 oz) mange-touts, trimmed
175 g (6 oz) fresh shiitake mushrooms, sliced, or 6 dried, soaked
for 20 minutes, drained and sliced (see p. 130)
salt
soy sauce
3 spring onions, chopped
250 g (8 oz) shelled prawns

1   Cook the noodles in a pan of boiling salted water until *al dente*.
2   Meanwhile, pound together the garlic and the base of the lemon grass stalks. Heat the oil in a wok over high heat. Add the ginger, garlic and lemon grass and stir-fry for 1 minute.
3   Stir in the mange-touts and mushrooms and season lightly with salt and soy sauce. Continue to stir-fry for another 2–3 minutes, then add the spring onions and prawns.
4   Add the drained noodles to the wok. Toss and stir-fry until some of the noodles are browning and the other ingredients are well distributed. Turn into a warmed bowl and serve.

Stuffed Onions

SERVES 6

6 Spanish onions, unpeeled
45 ml (3 tbsp) olive oil

Stuffing
150 g (5 oz) long grain rice, cooked
125 g (4 oz) blanched almonds, coarsely chopped
1 tsp ground allspice
½ tsp ground mace
4 tbsp chopped fresh parsley
salt and pepper

Cooking liquid
2 tbsp ground sumac
450 ml (¾ pint) boiling water
2 cloves garlic, crushed
juice of 1 lemon

1   Blanch the whole onions in a pan of boiling water for 45 minutes, then remove carefully and leave to cool. When you can handle them easily, take off the outer skin, cut off the root and a larger slice from the stem end. Leave the prepared onions upside down to drain.
2   Use a small sharp knife to detach the centre of the onion, lifting it out with a small spoon. The surrounding layers can then be removed quite easily. Work carefully or the onions may collapse, although they can be reformed round the stuffing.
3   Chop the flesh from the onions and combine with the other stuffing ingredients. Fill the onions, mounding up the stuffing. Put the oil into a baking tin in which the onions fit snugly, cover them with the "lids".
4   Stir the sumac into the boiling water, add the garlic and lemon juice. Pour the liquid around the onions. Bake in a preheated oven at 180°C, 350°F, gas 4 for 20 minutes, basting the onions from time to time. Lift them out carefully because they are quite fragile.

Stuffed Peppers

SERVES 6

6 large green peppers
30 ml (2 tbsp) olive oil
1 onion, chopped
250 g (8 oz) minced pork or beef
1 tomato, skinned and chopped
salt and pepper
¼ tsp grated nutmeg
¼ tsp nigella
50 g (2 oz) long grain rice
50 g (2 oz) yellow split peas, soaked for 1 hour
3 tbsp chopped fresh parsley
a few mint leaves, chopped
2 small pieces cassia or cinnamon
300 ml (½ pint) passata (puréed tomatoes)
150 ml (¼ pint) water
30 ml (2 tbsp) lemon juice
2 tsp sugar

1   Cut "lids" from the stem ends of the peppers, clean out the seeds and white membranes. Blanch the peppers in a pan of boiling water for 3 minutes. Put upside down to drain.
2   Heat the oil and sauté the onion for 3–4 minutes. Add the meat, tomato, salt, pepper, nutmeg and nigella and cook for 5 minutes. Add the rice, and the same volume of water, the drained split peas and herbs. Simmer for 10 minutes.
3   Stuff the peppers with this mixture. Stand them upright in a casserole in which they just fit, put on their lids, and set the pieces of cassia or cinnamon between them.
4   Dilute the passata with the water, stir in the lemon juice and sugar and pour over the peppers. Cover and bake in a preheated oven at 180°C, 350°F, gas 4 for 45 minutes. Serve hot.

Mediterranean Spiced Lentils

SERVES 4

250 g (8 oz) brown lentils, soaked for 1 hour
450 ml (¾ pint) water
¼ tsp mustard seeds
½ tsp crushed black peppercorns
½ tsp ground coriander
1 bay leaf
1 tsp salt
1 clove garlic, crushed
60 ml (4 tbsp) olive oil
1 small onion, sliced

1 Place the lentils in a pan with the water. Bring to the boil and then leave to simmer, partly covered, for 20 minutes.
2 Add the spices, bay leaf, salt and garlic and continue cooking until the lentils are soft and virtually reduced to a purée. There should be little water left. Beat with a wooden spoon to achieve a smoother purée if wished.
3 Heat the oil in a pan and sauté the onion until golden. Pour over the lentils and serve.

Dal

SERVES 4—6

Moong dal, the yellow split mung bean, is widely used in Indian cookery. It is easy to digest and absorbs other flavours well. The tadka is a traditional and effective way of flavouring foods.

300 g (10 oz) moong dal (split mung beans), washed
1 onion, chopped
3 cloves
1 small piece cinnamon stick
3 cardamoms, crushed
1 tsp ground turmeric
1 tsp ground cumin
1 litre (1¾ pints) water
salt

Tadka (aromatized butter)
60 ml (4 tbsp) clarified butter or oil
3 cloves garlic, finely sliced
½ tsp cayenne (optional)
2 tbsp chopped fresh coriander, to garnish

1 Put the beans in a pan with the onion, cloves, cinnamon, cardamom, turmeric, cumin and water. Bring to the boil, cover and simmer for 20 minutes.
2 Add salt to taste and continue to cook until the beans are soft, about 35 minutes, topping up with more hot water if necessary. Virtually all the liquid should have been absorbed. Discard the whole spices and transfer the beans to a warmed dish.
3 For the tadka, heat the butter in a pan over high heat. Stir in the garlic and cayenne and fry until the garlic starts to colour. Pour at once over the lentils. Garnish with coriander and serve.

Pilaf with Peas

SERVES 6

5 saffron threads
15 ml (1 tbsp) rose water
150 ml (¼ pint) single cream
½ tsp ground cinnamon
¼ tsp black pepper
¼ tsp ground cloves
salt
60 ml (4 tbsp) oil or clarified butter
½ tsp ground cumin
2 curry leaves
small piece of fresh ginger, peeled and finely chopped
350 g (12 oz) shelled peas
350 g (12 oz) basmati rice
600 ml (1 pint) water

1 Crush the saffron and blend with the rose water. Stir the rose water into the cream together with the cinnamon, pepper, cloves and a little salt.
2 Heat the oil in a large pan, stir in the cumin, curry leaves and ginger.
3 Add the peas and rice. Cook, stirring, until the rice starts to turn brown. Add the water, bring to the boil, then simmer uncovered, until virtually all the water is absorbed.
4 Pour over the spiced cream. Cover with a piece of foil and the lid, then put over the lowest possible heat and leave for 20 minutes.

Malabar Rice

SERVES 6—8

Pilafs flavoured with whole spices are found in many parts of India; this one comes from Malabar, home of cardamom and pepper, and makes the perfect accompaniment to braised chicken or lamb. Except for the cumin seeds the spices are not eaten, but you won't come to harm if you accidentally chew on any of the others.

500 g (1 lb) long grain rice
900 ml (1½ pints) water
30 ml (2 tbsp) vegetable oil or clarified butter
1 large onion, chopped
8 green cardamoms
12 cm (5 in) cinnamon stick
8 cloves
1 tsp cumin seeds
12 black peppercorns
2 tsp salt

1 Wash the rice and leave to soak for 30 minutes in the water.
2 Heat the oil in a heavy pan and fry the onion until golden. Bruise the cardamoms lightly and break the cinnamon into three. Add them to the onion with the cloves, cumin and peppercorns. Fry gently for about 30 seconds until the spices are slightly puffed and browned.

3 Drain the rice, reserve the water and put the rice into the pan. Fry for about 3 minutes until the rice becomes translucent, then add the water and salt. Stir frequently and bring to the boil.

4 Reduce the heat to very low. Cover the pan and simmer for 20 minutes or until all the water is absorbed. The surface of the rice will be covered with tiny holes.

5 Turn off the heat, replace the lid and leave the rice to steam for another 10 minutes. (It will in fact stay warm for about 20 minutes if left covered.)

6 When ready to serve, turn out the rice on to a warmed platter with a wooden fork (a spoon might break the grains), fluffing it as you do so.

Steamed Aubergine with Sesame Sauce

SERVES 4 – 6

This dish tastes best if the sauce is made a day in advance so that the flavours have time to blend. Try at least to make it several hours ahead, and keep covered at room temperature. The aubergine can be served hot, but I prefer it at room temperature.

handful of coriander leaves
3 cloves garlic, crushed with salt
30 ml (2 tbsp) Chinese sesame paste
30 ml (2 tbsp) sesame oil
45 ml (3 tbsp) light soy sauce
30 ml (2 tbsp) rice vinegar
30 ml (2 tbsp) dry sherry
5 ml (1 tsp) chilli sauce
¼ tsp ground fagara
salt
4 long aubergines

1 For the sauce, chop the coriander coarsely in a food processor. Add the remaining ingredients, except the aubergines, to the coriander. Process to a thick smooth sauce. If the sauce thickens too much while standing, thin it with a little water.

2 Peel alternate strips from the aubergines, sprinkle with salt and leave to drain for 45 minutes.

3 Rinse, then steam the aubergines for about 35 minutes until soft. Cut the aubergines into strips and pour the sauce over them just before serving.

Hungarian Paprika Potatoes

SERVES 6

These potatoes are good with chops and sausages.

25 g (1 oz) butter
3 shallots, sliced
1½ tsp paprika
2 large tomatoes, skinned and chopped
salt
1 kg (2 lb) potatoes, thickly sliced
300 ml (½ pint) stock
150 ml (¼ pint) sour cream

1 Melt the butter in a flameproof casserole and stew the shallots until soft. Stir in the paprika and cook for a few minutes.

2 Add the tomatoes, salt to taste, and potatoes. Cover with the stock and sour cream.

3 Cover and cook in a preheated oven at 200°C, 400°F, gas 6 for about 1 hour, until the liquid is almost absorbed.

Spinach and Walnut Pasty with Tahina Sauce

SERVES 4

1.5 kg (3 lb) spinach, washed
40 g (1½ oz) butter
3 onions, sliced
75 g (3 oz) walnuts, finely chopped
½ tsp ground allspice
½ tsp ground cinnamon
salt and pepper
250 g (8 oz) frozen puff pastry, thawed
1 egg yolk

Sauce
90 ml (6 tbsp) tahina
30 ml (2 tbsp) sunflower oil
90–120 ml (6–8 tbsp) thick natural yogurt
lemon juice to taste

1 Cook the spinach in a pan with only the water clinging to the leaves for 4–5 minutes. Squeeze out all moisture and chop.

2 Melt the butter in a pan and stew the onions until soft. Mix together the onions, spinach, nuts, spices and seasoning.

3 Roll out the pastry to a large square, 25–30 cm (10–12 in). Put the filling in the centre, fold up the corners to meet in the middle and then pinch the seams closed.

4 Place on a baking sheet and brush with the egg yolk beaten with 15 ml (1 tbsp) water. Bake in a preheated oven at 220°C, 425°F, gas 7 for about 30 minutes or until golden.

5 Meanwhile, prepare the sauce. Blend all the ingredients to a smooth, quite liquid consistency and serve separately.

Barley with Mushrooms

SERVES 4

75 g (3 oz) butter
2 onions, sliced
250 g (8 oz) pearl barley
½ tsp dill seeds or ¼ tsp celery seeds
600 ml (1 pint) stock
salt and pepper
250 g (8 oz) mushrooms
150 ml (¼ pint) natural yogurt
paprika

1 Melt half the butter in an earthenware or cast-iron casserole and stew the onions until soft.
2 Stir in the barley and cook for a few minutes to coat well with the butter. Stir in the dill seeds and pour over the stock. Taste for seasoning.
3 Cover tightly and bake in a preheated oven at 180°C, 350°F, gas 4 for about 1 hour until the barley is soft and the stock absorbed.
4 Meanwhile, quarter or thickly slice the mushrooms. Melt the remaining butter in a pan and sauté the mushrooms briefly.
5 Stir the mushrooms carefully into the barley. Add the yogurt, sprinkle with paprika and serve.

Potatoes with Bacon and Juniper

SERVES 4

A satisfying potato stew which can be varied by using different spices.

15 g (½ oz) butter
4 shallots, chopped
175 g (6 oz) smoked bacon, diced
500 g (1 lb) potatoes, peeled and sliced
salt and pepper
½ tsp juniper berries, crushed
150 ml (¼ pint) water

1 Melt the butter in a pan and cook the shallots slowly until soft. Add the bacon and cook a few minutes more.
2 Put a layer of shallots and bacon in the bottom of an earthenware casserole, followed by a layer of potatoes. Season well with salt and pepper and put in some of the juniper. Add more layers, finishing with potatoes. Pour over the water.
3 Cover tightly with foil and then the lid. Cook in a preheated oven at 160°C, 325°F, gas 3 for 1½–2 hours – the potatoes will not come to any harm if left for the longer time.

VARIATIONS

◆ Use ground allspice instead of juniper and add a layer or two of sliced tomatoes if wished.
◆ Use ¼ tsp ground celery seeds or ½ tsp ground fenugreek in place of the juniper and add some sliced parsnip to the potatoes.

Falafel

SERVES 4

Falafel are perhaps the most popular street food of the Middle East. They are tricky to make without a food processor because the paste must be smooth enough not to disintegrate when fried. If you have trouble making the falafel adhere, add a tablespoon or two of flour to the mixture.

250 g (8 oz) chick peas, soaked for 36 hours
1 large onion, chopped
3 cloves garlic, crushed
handful of fresh parsley or coriander, chopped
1 tsp ground coriander
1 tsp ground cumin
¼ tsp cayenne (optional)
salt
¼ tsp baking powder
oil for deep frying

1 Drain, rinse the chick peas and grind to a purée in a food processor. As they crumble, add the onion, garlic and parsley, and continue processing to a fine purée. (You will need to stop and start the processor several times and scrape around the sides of the bowl.)
2 Blend in the spices, salt and baking powder. Leave the mixture to rest in a cool place for at least 1 hour.
3 Form the mixture into small balls, each the size of a walnut. Flatten them slightly and leave to rest again for 15 minutes.
4 Deep fry the falafel for 3–4 minutes, turning once. Drain on kitchen paper towels and serve with tahina sauce (p. 56), a tomato salad and slices of pitta bread.

Shiitake Mushrooms with Ginger, Fagara and Garlic

SERVES 4

These Japanese mushrooms have a delicious flavour and are available from Oriental stores and some supermarkets.

350 g (12 oz) fresh shiitake mushrooms
60 ml (4 tbsp) oil
small piece of fresh ginger, peeled and finely chopped
3 cloves garlic, crushed
1 tsp fagara, crushed
Chinese or ordinary chives, chopped, to garnish

1 Wipe the mushrooms and cut them in pieces.
2 Heat the oil in a frying pan and fry the ginger, garlic and fagara for 1–2 minutes.
3 Add the mushrooms and sauté for 4–5 minutes. Serve garnished with Chinese or ordinary chives.

Mushrooms in Sour Cream

SERVES 6

40 g (1½ oz) butter
1 small onion, sliced
500 g (1 lb) mushrooms, sliced
½ tsp caraway seeds
salt and pepper
150 ml (¼ pint) sour cream
paprika

1   Melt the butter in a pan and stew the onion until soft.
2   Add the mushrooms and caraway seeds and season to taste. Simmer for 10–12 minutes.
3   Stir in the sour cream, heat through and serve sprinkled with paprika.

Courgette Fritters

SERVES 6

15 g (½ oz) butter
1 large onion, grated
500 g (1 lb) courgettes, peeled and grated
125 g (4 oz) curd cheese
4 eggs
½ tsp ground cumin
¼ tsp nigella
salt and pepper
oil for frying

1   Melt the butter in a pan and sauté the onion briefly. Add the courgettes and cook for 2–3 minutes. Drain well.
2   Mix the vegetables with the cheese, eggs, spices and season to taste.
3   Heat enough oil to cover the frying pan to a depth of 5 mm (¼ in). Spoon in the mixture, 1 tbsp at a time, keeping the fritters well apart. Cook until golden brown, 3–4 minutes, turning once. Drain on kitchen paper towels and serve.

Onion Purée

SERVES 4

125 g (4 oz) butter
750 g (1½ lb) onions, finely sliced
1 tsp salt
2 tsp ras el hanout (pp. 96–7)
45 ml (3 tbsp) honey
30 ml (2 tbsp) sherry vinegar

1   Heat the butter in a pan until a deep golden colour. Put in the onions, salt and ras el hanout and stir to mix.
2   Cover and cook slowly over a heat diffuser for 30 minutes, stirring from time to time.
3   Add the honey and sherry vinegar and cook, uncovered, for another 30 minutes, stirring the mixture frequently.

Aubergine and Sesame Purée

SERVES 4—6

A natural combination; the vegetable and the spice complement each other perfectly. In the Middle East, tahina paste and garlic are blended with aubergine purée to make *Baba Ghanoush*. I have made a simple Oriental version using Chinese sesame paste.

2 large aubergines
2 cloves garlic, crushed with salt
22–30 ml (1½–2 tbsp) Chinese sesame paste
15–30 ml (1–2 tbsp) Oriental sesame oil
¾ tsp Chinese five-spice powder (pp. 72–3)
juice of 2 lemons
safflower or paprika, to garnish

1   Wipe the aubergines and prick a few times with a fork. Place in a baking dish and cook in a preheated oven at 180 °C, 350°F, gas 4 for 20–30 minutes until soft.
2   Cut off the stalks, then peel when cool enough to handle. Squeeze out any excess liquid and chop the flesh roughly.
3   Purée the aubergine, garlic, sesame paste, sesame oil and Chinese five-spice powder in a food processor, or pound well in a mortar. Add lemon juice to obtain a smooth purée and to your taste – the juice of two lemons should be about right.
4   Serve at room temperature, sprinkled with a little safflower or paprika.

Spinach with Ginger

SERVES 2

500 g (1 lb) spinach
15 ml (1 tbsp) sunflower oil
¼ tsp ground cumin
2 mild green chillies, seeded and sliced
1 tsp Japanese pickled ginger, shredded
salt

1   Cut the spinach leaves into broad ribbons. Wash, then blanch them in a large pan of boiling water for 1 minute.
2   Drain and run cold water over the spinach until cool. Press thoroughly to extract excess water; it must be dry before frying.
3   Heat a wok or large frying pan to a high temperature. Add the oil and, when smoking, stir in the cumin and chillies and toss for a few seconds.
4   Add the spinach, tossing rapidly to separate the pieces and to coat with the oil. Sprinkle on the ginger and a little salt. Stir to blend and serve immediately. The whole frying operation should take only about 1 minute – if the spinach cooks too slowly it becomes watery.

Chakchouka

SERVES 4

This is a Tunisian dish, now popular throughout the Middle East. It is usually made with eggs broken into hollows in the vegetables, then cooked until set. I prefer to use merguez sausages instead.

30 ml (2 tbsp) olive oil
2 green, red or yellow peppers, seeded and sliced
2 onions, sliced
4 merguez sausages, sliced
4 large tomatoes, peeled and quartered
salt and pepper
5 ml (1 tsp) harissa (pp. 94–5)

1　Heat the oil in a pan and sauté the peppers and onions until nearly soft.
2　Add the sausages, cook for a few minutes, then stir in the tomatoes. Season with salt, pepper and harissa to taste.
3　Cook slowly for a further 8–10 minutes until the vegetables have blended.

Braised Leeks

SERVES 3–4

500 g (1 lb) leeks
25 g (1 oz) butter
½ tsp Chinese five-spice powder (pp. 72–3)
¼ tsp ground galangal
30 ml (2 tbsp) vegetable stock

1　Slice the leeks, but not too finely.
2　Melt the butter in a heavy pan just large enough to take the leeks, stir in the spices and fry for a few minutes. Add the leeks, turn and stir to coat them in the spiced butter. Put in the stock.
3　Cover tightly, turn the heat to low and cook for 20 minutes.

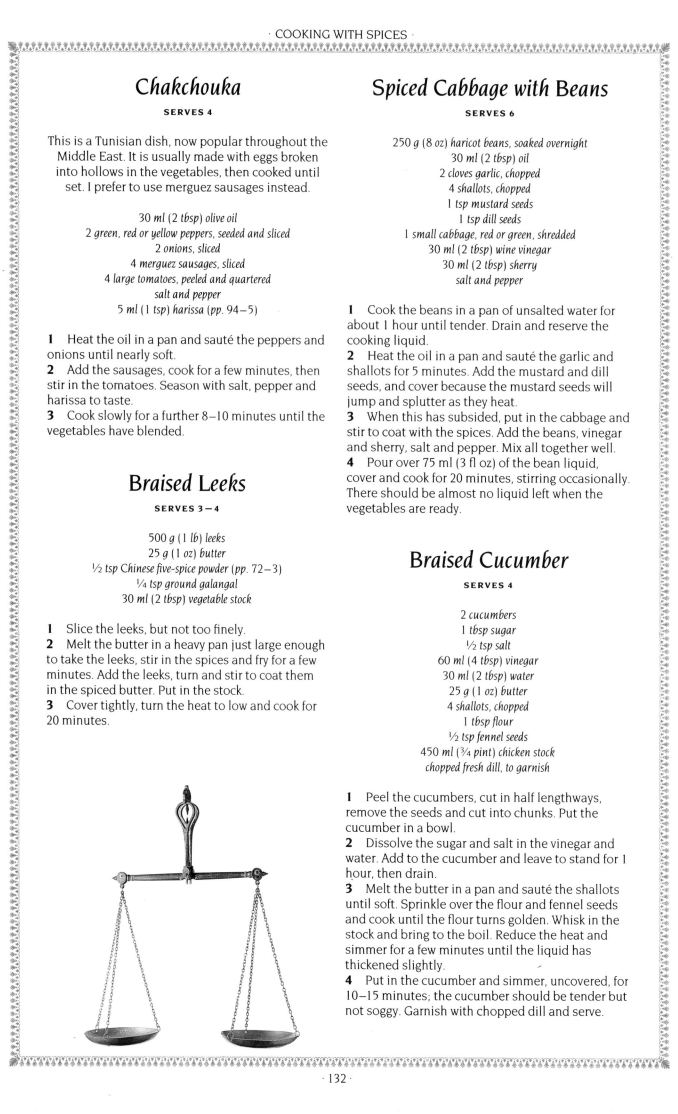

Spiced Cabbage with Beans

SERVES 6

250 g (8 oz) haricot beans, soaked overnight
30 ml (2 tbsp) oil
2 cloves garlic, chopped
4 shallots, chopped
1 tsp mustard seeds
1 tsp dill seeds
1 small cabbage, red or green, shredded
30 ml (2 tbsp) wine vinegar
30 ml (2 tbsp) sherry
salt and pepper

1　Cook the beans in a pan of unsalted water for about 1 hour until tender. Drain and reserve the cooking liquid.
2　Heat the oil in a pan and sauté the garlic and shallots for 5 minutes. Add the mustard and dill seeds, and cover because the mustard seeds will jump and splutter as they heat.
3　When this has subsided, put in the cabbage and stir to coat with the spices. Add the beans, vinegar and sherry, salt and pepper. Mix all together well.
4　Pour over 75 ml (3 fl oz) of the bean liquid, cover and cook for 20 minutes, stirring occasionally. There should be almost no liquid left when the vegetables are ready.

Braised Cucumber

SERVES 4

2 cucumbers
1 tbsp sugar
½ tsp salt
60 ml (4 tbsp) vinegar
30 ml (2 tbsp) water
25 g (1 oz) butter
4 shallots, chopped
1 tbsp flour
½ tsp fennel seeds
450 ml (¾ pint) chicken stock
chopped fresh dill, to garnish

1　Peel the cucumbers, cut in half lengthways, remove the seeds and cut into chunks. Put the cucumber in a bowl.
2　Dissolve the sugar and salt in the vinegar and water. Add to the cucumber and leave to stand for 1 hour, then drain.
3　Melt the butter in a pan and sauté the shallots until soft. Sprinkle over the flour and fennel seeds and cook until the flour turns golden. Whisk in the stock and bring to the boil. Reduce the heat and simmer for a few minutes until the liquid has thickened slightly.
4　Put in the cucumber and simmer, uncovered, for 10–15 minutes; the cucumber should be tender but not soggy. Garnish with chopped dill and serve.

Salads

Olive, Pomegranate and Walnut Salad

SERVES 4

This is a version of a salad served at lunch to a group of visiting food enthusiasts by the women's council of Gaziantep in Southeastern Turkey. It is a town surrounded by olive and pistachio groves and noted for the variety of its kebabs and the excellence of its baklava. The lunch, a buffet of some 30 dishes, was remarkable for its refinement and richness.

2 large pomegranates
125 g (4 oz) green olives, stoned and chopped
bunch of coriander leaves, chopped
6–8 spring onions, chopped
125 g (4 oz) walnuts, coarsely chopped

Dressing
22 ml (1½ tbsp) lemon juice
45 ml (3 tbsp) olive oil
pinch of red pepper
salt

1   Cut open the pomegranates and extract the seeds. Combine with the olives, coriander, spring onions and walnuts.
2   Make a piquant dressing with the remaining ingredients. Pour over the salad, toss and serve.

VARIATION
◆   A few shredded young sorrel leaves make a pleasant addition.

Savoy Cabbage Salad

SERVES 4

1 small Savoy cabbage
50 g (2 oz) pine nuts, toasted

Dressing
60 ml (4 tbsp) olive oil
30 ml (2 tbsp) wine vinegar
¼ tsp poppy seeds
pinch of celery seeds
¼ tsp paprika
2 tsp soft brown sugar
salt

1   Remove the large central stalks from the cabbage leaves, then shred finely.
2   Blanch the cabbage for 1 minute in boiling water, drain and refresh under cold water. Drain thoroughly and cool. Put the cabbage and pine nuts in a bowl.
3   For the dressing, whisk together all the other ingredients. Pour over the salad, toss and serve.

Indian Carrot Salad

SERVES 4 – 6

This salad is based on a recipe in Julie Sahni's *Classic Indian Vegetarian Cooking.*

500 g (1 lb) carrots
15 ml (1 tbsp) mustard oil
1 tsp mustard seeds
2 green chillies, seeded and chopped
good pinch of ground asafoetida
2 tsp sugar
1 tsp curry powder (pp. 80–1)
squeeze of lemon juice
pinch of ground cloves
salt
60 ml (4 tbsp) thick natural yogurt
2 tbsp roasted cashew nuts, chopped
fresh mint leaves, to garnish

1   Slice the carrots very thinly.
2   Heat the oil in a large frying pan and add the mustard seeds. Cover with a lid when they start to jump about. As the spattering subsides, add the chillies, asafoetida, sugar and curry powder. Shake the pan and stir for a few seconds.
3   When the sugar dissolves, add the carrots and toss well to separate the slices and coat them with the oil and spices. Cook for 3–4 minutes, then transfer to a bowl and leave to cool.
4   Stir the lemon juice, cloves and salt into the yogurt and toss the carrots in the dressing. Sprinkle the nuts and a few mint leaves over the salad. Serve at room temperature.

Beetroot Salad

SERVES 4

350 g (12 oz) beetroot

Dressing
45 ml (3 tbsp) wine vinegar
90 ml (6 tbsp) olive oil
2 tsp sugar
½ tsp fennel seeds or ¼ tsp celery seeds
pinch of ground ginger
4 spring onions, chopped
salt

1   Cook the unpeeled beetroot in a pan of boiling salted water until tender. Drain, skin and cut in julienne strips.
2   For the dressing, whisk together all the other ingredients. Pour the dressing over the beetroot and leave to stand for 1 hour for the flavours to blend before serving.

Bean and Pasta Salad

SERVES 8–10

125 g (4 oz) dried haricot beans
125 g (4 oz) dried red kidney beans
125 g (4 oz) flageolets
350 g (12 oz) pasta shells or bows
125 g (4 oz) French beans
1 large clove garlic, finely chopped
large handful of assorted chopped fresh herbs, such as parsley,
chives, tarragon, basil, chervil, sweet cicely
about 120 ml (8 tbsp) olive oil
30–45 ml (2–3 tbsp) wine vinegar
salt and black pepper
10 g (2 tsp) mustard

1 Soak the dried beans separately for 2–3 hours. Cook the beans separately in boiling water until just tender, fast boiling the red beans for the first ten minutes. Do not allow them to become too soft. Drain and leave to cool.
2 Cook the pasta shells in a pan of boiling salted water until *al dente*; again it is important not to overcook them, because soft pasta does not take well to being dressed and served cold. When ready, drain and cool under cold running water.
3 Briefly cook the French beans in boiling salted water. Drain, cool and cut in two.
4 Combine the pasta and cooked dried beans in a large serving bowl with the garlic and herbs.
5 For the dressing, whisk together the oil, vinegar, salt, pepper and mustard. Pour the dressing over the salad.
6 Add the French beans and toss carefully. Chill the salad for 1–2 hours before serving.

Cucumber Salad

SERVES 4–6

An Oriental salad influenced by one I enjoyed in a Korean restaurant. Use sansho if you want a hot chilli flavour; fagara for a milder taste.

1 tbsp sugar
1 tsp salt
60 ml (4 tbsp) wine or rice vinegar
½ tsp sansho or crushed fagara
30 ml (2 tbsp) sesame oil
1 cucumber, finely sliced
1 tbsp black sesame seeds, toasted

1 Whisk the sugar and salt into the vinegar until dissolved. Add the sansho or fagara and oil.
2 Pour over the cucumber, sprinkle with sesame seeds and serve at room temperature.

VARIATIONS
◆ Toasted white sesame seeds can be used instead, but the black look more dramatic.
◆ About 5–10 ml (1–2 tsp) light soy sauce can be added to the dressing; finely sliced onion can be added to the cucumber.

Gado Gado

SERVES 4

An inexpensive Indonesian salad that is excellent on its own or as an accompaniment to a main course. The selection of vegetables can be varied to suit your taste, but do keep the bean sprouts for an authentic dish.

250 g (8 oz) bean sprouts, washed
250 g (8 oz) cabbage, shredded
250 g (8 oz) leek, cut in julienne strips
250 g (8 oz) carrots, cut in julienne strips
250 g (8 oz) celery, cut in julienne strips
1 hard-boiled egg, finely chopped, to garnish

Sauce
1 clove garlic
1 small onion
1 tsp trassi (pp. 154–5)
1 tsp dark brown sugar
1 small ball tamarind
30 ml (2 tbsp) coconut cream
30 ml (2 tbsp) milk
60 ml (4 tbsp) crunchy peanut butter
½ tsp ground cumin
½ tsp chilli powder (optional)
½ tsp ground lemon grass
5 ml (1 tsp) dark soy sauce

1 Put the bean sprouts in a large serving dish.
2 Steam the other vegetables until just tender. Arrange them on top of the bean sprouts.
3 For the sauce, crush the garlic and onion to a paste with a pestle and mortar.
4 Wrap the trassi in foil and heat it in a dry pan or moderate oven (180°C, 350°F, gas 4) for a few minutes, then crumble and mix it with the sugar. Dissolve the tamarind in 15–30 ml (1–2 tbsp) water. Stir the coconut cream into the milk to make a thick coconut milk.
5 Blend the sauce ingredients together to make a sauce thick enough to coat the vegetables and not run to the bottom of the dish. Pour over the vegetables and garnish with the chopped egg.

Onion Salad with Sumac

SERVES 4

A simple side dish that is encountered all through the Middle East.

2 onions, thinly sliced
½ tsp ground sumac
salt

1 Put the onions in a bowl and sprinkle with sumac and a little salt.
2 Leave to stand for 30 minutes before serving.

*Gado Gado with tamarind, cumin, chilli powder and lemon grass, and **Onion Salad with Sumac** in the foreground.*

Desserts

Spiced Cream Cheese

SERVES 4

250 g (8 oz) cream cheese
150 g (5 oz) thick natural yogurt
125 g (4 oz) caster sugar
¼ tsp saffron threads
30 ml (2 tbsp) hot milk
¼ tsp grated nutmeg
seeds of 6 cardamom pods, crushed

1 Combine the cream cheese, yogurt and caster sugar in a bowl.
2 Crush the saffron and infuse in the hot milk for 10 minutes, then strain.
3 Stir the saffron milk and nutmeg into the cream cheese. Sprinkle the crushed cardamom seeds on top and serve cold.

Kheer (Indian Rice Pudding)

SERVES 4 — 6

Do not think of this as a Western rice pudding; the two dishes are utterly different. Kheer is cooked for several hours so that the rice breaks down and the pudding has the consistency of a thick cream.

1.2 litres (2 pints) milk
75 g (3 oz) long grain rice, washed
125 g (4 oz) sugar
75 g (3 oz) raisins
40 g (1½ oz) dried apricots, cut into small pieces
seeds of 6 cardamoms, bruised
2 cm (¾ in) cinnamon stick
40 g (1½ oz) blanched, slivered almonds or pistachios
10 ml (2 tsp) rose water

1 Boil the milk and add the rice. Stir over a high heat for 1 minute, then turn the heat as low as possible and continue to cook for 10 minutes, stirring all the time. Leave to cook for a further 1½ hours, stirring occasionally.
2 Add the sugar, raisins, apricots, cardamom and cinnamon. Cook for about 1 hour, stirring from time to time. The dried fruit will plump up and the pudding will thicken. Stir in most of the almonds and cook for another 30 minutes.
3 Leave until cold, then mix in the rose water. The kheer will now have a thick pouring consistency.
4 Put the kheer into a shallow glass bowl or individual bowls, sprinkle the top with the remaining almonds and chill. Kheer may also be decorated with edible gold or silver leaf, bought from Indian grocers.

Orange and Cardamom Salad

SERVES 6

10 oranges
30 ml (2 tbsp) orange flower water
½ tsp ground cardamom
generous pinch of grated nutmeg
50 g (2 oz) sugar
125 ml (4 fl oz) water
icing sugar

1 Peel the oranges, removing all pith and reserving the peel from one or two. Divide into segments. Put them into a serving bowl and sprinkle with the orange flower water and spices.
2 Take the reserved peel, make sure no pith is adhering to it, and cut into julienne strips. Blanch in boiling water for 3 minutes.
3 Melt the sugar in the water in a pan. Add the blanched strips of orange peel and poach slowly for 4–5 minutes. Drain the strips on a wire rack.
4 To serve, scatter the peel over the oranges and sift over a dusting of icing sugar.

Bananas with Cinnamon and Rum

SERVES 4

4 ripe bananas
25 g (1 oz) butter
1 tsp ground cinnamon
75 ml (5 tbsp) rum or whisky
45 ml (3 tbsp) clear honey
50 g (2 oz) walnuts, coarsely chopped

1 Cut the bananas into thick slices. Melt the butter in a pan and fry the banana slices until soft. Lift the bananas out and keep them warm on a serving dish.
2 Add the cinnamon to the butter, then the rum and honey and cook until the sauce thickens slightly. Stir in the walnuts.
3 Pour the sauce over the warm banana slices and serve with cream.

Clementines in Brandy

MAKES 1 KG (2 LB)

This recipe is based on "Clementines in Armagnac" from Jane Grigson's *Fruit Book*. They make an excellent dessert or sweetmeat.

1 kg (2 lb) small clementines
625 g (1¼ lb) sugar
1 vanilla pod
1 litre (1¾ pints) water
brandy or armagnac

1   Prick the fruit a few times with a needle.
2   To make a syrup, heat the sugar, vanilla pod and water in a pan. When the sugar has dissolved, bring to the boil and boil for 3–4 minutes.
3   Put in the clementines, bring back to the boil, then simmer very gently for about 30 minutes. The time depends on the size of the fruit – large fruit may need a little longer. If the skins start to split they are certainly ready.
4   Lift out the fruit and put into warmed preserving jars. Add brandy or armagnac almost to cover the fruit.
5   Boil down the syrup by half and use to top up the jars. Divide the vanilla pod between them.
6   Put a clean stone or a crumpled piece of foil on top of the fruits so that they are totally immersed in the liquid. Seal the jars and keep for 2–3 weeks before eating.

VARIATIONS

◆   Use 5–6 bruised cardamom pods instead of the vanilla, but do not put them into the syrup until the fruit is added. Whisky is a good alternative to brandy with cardamom.
◆   Clear spirit such as vodka, or continental preserving spirit such as plain *alcool blanc*, can be used instead of brandy.

Spiced Fruit Salad

SERVES 4

3 oranges, peeled and cut in segments
2 bananas, peeled and sliced
½ small melon, cut in cubes
4 apricots, quartered
4 greengage plums, quartered
2 peaches, sliced
2 tbsp vanilla sugar (p. 60)
juice of 2 oranges
juice of 1 lemon
15 ml (1 tbsp) orange flower water
½ tsp ground cinnamon
¼ tsp ground coriander

1   Put the fruit in a serving bowl.
2   Dissolve the sugar in the fruit juices. Stir in the orange flower water and spices.
3   Pour the spiced fruit juice over the fruit and mix carefully. Chill for 2–3 hours before serving.

Poppy Seed Ice Cream

SERVES 4

300 ml (½ pint) milk
1 vanilla pod
3 egg yolks
50 g (2 oz) sugar
75 g (3 oz) poppy seeds
125 g (4 oz) honey
150 ml (¼ pint) double cream

1   Put the milk and vanilla pod in a pan and bring to the boil. Remove from the heat and leave to infuse for 10 minutes.
2   Whisk the egg yolks and sugar together until thick and cream coloured in a bowl set over a pan of simmering water.
3   Remove the vanilla pod from the milk and pour the milk on to the egg and sugar. Stir constantly until the mixture thickens enough to coat the back of a spoon, but do not let it boil or it may curdle.
4   When the custard is thick enough to leave a clear trail from a wooden spoon on the bottom of the bowl, remove the bowl to a cool surface.
5   Toast the poppy seeds in a dry pan. Stir the seeds and honey into the custard and leave to cool.
6   Whip the cream to soft peaks and fold into the custard. Freeze in an ice cream machine or a shallow container, beating the ice cream after 1–2 hours, then freeze until firm.

Vanilla and Cardamom Ice Cream

SERVES 4

300 ml (½ pint) milk
1 vanilla pod
150 ml (¼ pint) double cream
6 green cardamoms, crushed
4 egg yolks
125 g (4 oz) sugar

1   Put the milk and vanilla pod in a pan and bring to the boil. Remove from the heat and leave to infuse for 10 minutes. Remove the vanilla pod.
2   Heat the cream with the cardamom pods and leave to infuse.
3   Whisk the egg yolks and sugar in a double boiler or in a bowl set over a pan of boiling water until thick and pale coloured. Add the warm milk and stir briskly to blend. Keep stirring until the mixture thickens.
4   Remove the cardamom pods from the cream, it doesn't matter about the seeds, and add the cream to the custard. Cook and stir for a further 10 minutes until the mixture thickens again.
5   Freeze in an ice cream machine or a shallow container, beating the ice cream after 1–2 hours, then freeze until firm.

Breads, cakes & biscuits

Onion and Juniper Bread

A very quick and easy loaf that is best eaten soon after it is made. Fennel, caraway, celery seeds, anise and cumin all combine well with the onion in this recipe if you want to try a different flavour.

175 ml (6 fl oz) milk
1 tsp salt
15 g (½ oz) butter
½ packet easy-blend dried yeast or 7 g (¼ oz) dried yeast
350 g (12 oz) strong white flour
175 ml (6 fl oz) warm water
2 tbsp finely chopped onion
2 tbsp finely chopped juniper berries

1 Heat the milk in a pan and stir in the salt and butter until dissolved.
2 Sprinkle the easy-blend yeast over the flour. Prove ordinary dried yeast in the warm water. Stir the water into the flour, then the milk.
3 Scatter over the onion and juniper and stir to mix well. The dough should be quite soft and batter-like; it is easily mixed with a wooden spoon.
4 Cover and leave in a warm place to rise until it has doubled in bulk – about 1 hour. Beat thoroughly for 1–2 minutes, then pour the dough into a greased 20 cm (8 in) loaf tin.
5 Bake in a preheated oven at 180°C, 350°F, gas 4 for about 1 hour. The loaf should sound hollow when tapped on the bottom.

Churek

This bread comes from the republics of the Caucasus, but a similar anise-flavoured bread is popular throughout Morocco.

½ packet easy-blend yeast or 7 g (¼ oz) dried yeast
500 g (1 lb) strong white flour
1 tsp salt
1 tbsp ground anise
50 g (2 oz) butter, melted
300 ml (½ pint) warm milk
1 egg, beaten
sesame seeds

1 If using easy-blend yeast, stir it into the flour with the salt and anise. Prove ordinary dried yeast in a little warm water, then stir into the flour.
2 Add the melted butter and enough of the warm milk to make a soft dough. If it is too firm, add a little more milk or warm water.
3 Knead the dough on a floured surface for about 5 minutes or until smooth. (This can also be done in a food processor or a food mixer with a dough attachment.)

4 Put the dough in a lightly oiled bowl, and cover with clingfilm or a cloth. Leave to rise until it has doubled in bulk – about 2 hours.
5 Knock back and divide the dough in two. Form each one into a round. Alternatively, divide each piece of dough in three, form each third into a rope and plait them, pinching the ends together.
6 Put the loaves on greased baking sheets, cover and leave to rise for about 45 minutes. Brush the top of the bread with beaten egg and sprinkle thickly with sesame seeds.
7 Bake in a preheated oven at 180°C, 350°F, gas 4 for 35–40 minutes until the bread sounds hollow when tapped on the bottom.

VARIATIONS

◆ Substitute the seeds scraped from a vanilla pod for the anise and sprinkle the top of the bread with flaked almonds.
◆ Use 1 tbsp mahlab instead of the anise.

Arab Bread

½ packet easy-blend yeast or 7 g (¼ oz) dried yeast
500 g (1 lb) strong white flour
1 tsp salt
about 450 ml (¾ pint) warm water
olive oil and zahtar (pp. 96–7) or 1 beaten egg with nigella,
poppy seeds or sesame

1 Sprinkle the easy-blend yeast over the flour with the salt. Prove ordinary dried yeast in a little of the warm water, then stir into the flour. Add enough water to mix to a fairly stiff dough.
2 Knead the dough on a floured surface until elastic. Put the dough in a lightly oiled bowl and cover with clingfilm or a cloth. Leave to rise until it has doubled in bulk – about 1½ hours.
3 Knock back and divide the dough into two. Form the two pieces into round loaves and put them on a greased baking sheet. Cover and leave to rise for 30 minutes.
4 Either spread the tops thickly with a paste of olive oil and zahtar or brush with beaten egg and sprinkle with one of the spices.
5 Bake in a preheated oven at 200°C, 400°F, gas 6 for 8–10 minutes, then reduce the temperature to 160°C, 325°F, gas 3 for a further 15–20 minutes.

Spice Bread

Breads such as this are common throughout Europe. The spicing may vary according to the country, but the general principles are the same. Spices, dried fruit and nuts may be changed to suit your own preference.

175 g (6 oz) butter
75 g (3 oz) vanilla sugar (p. 60)
2 eggs
300 g (10 oz) strong white flour
2 tsp baking powder
50 g (2 oz) raisins
50 g (2 oz) almonds, chopped
50 g (2 oz) candied orange peel, chopped
50 g (2 oz) candied citron or lemon peel, chopped
1 tsp anise seeds
1 tsp ground cinnamon
½ tsp ground cloves

1 Cream the butter and sugar together in a bowl until pale. Beat in the eggs, one at a time.
2 Sift the flour and baking powder and stir in all the dried fruits and spices. Stir half the flour mixture into the bowl and mix well. Add the remaining flour gradually, and a little milk if the dough is too dry.
3 Knead the dough briefly on a floured surface until it can hold its shape. Cut it in two and place in two small 500 g (1 lb) buttered loaf tins.
4 Bake in a preheated oven at 180°C, 350°F, gas 4 for about 40 minutes – a skewer inserted in the centre should come out clean.

Swedish Limpa Bread

300 ml (½ pint) water
1 tbsp caraway seeds
1 tbsp fennel seeds
1½ tbsp grated orange rind
75 g (3 oz) soft brown sugar
1 packet easy-blend yeast or 15 g (½ oz) dried yeast
500 g (1 lb) strong plain white flour
2 tsp salt
300 ml (½ pint) milk
250 g (8 oz) rye flour

1 Bring the water to the boil and pour it over the caraway, fennel, orange rind and sugar.
2 When it has cooled to tepid, stir in the ordinary dried yeast, if using, and leave to prove. Mix the easy-blend yeast into the white flour with the salt.
3 Add the white flour to the water with the milk and mix. Add as much rye flour as necessary to make a fairly stiff dough.
4 Knead the dough well on a floured surface for about 10 minutes until quite elastic.
5 Put the dough in a lightly oiled bowl, and cover with clingfilm or a cloth. Leave to rise until it has doubled in bulk – about 2 hours.

6 Knock back and form the dough into two round loaves. Put them on greased baking sheets, cover and leave to rise for about 1 hour.
7 Bake in a preheated oven at 180°C, 350°F, gas 4 for 35–40 minutes.

Saffron Bread

½ tsp saffron threads
30 ml (2 tbsp) hot water
300 ml (½ pint) milk
1 packet easy-blend yeast or 15 g (½ oz) dried yeast
50 g (2 oz) butter, melted
4 tbsp sugar
½ tsp salt
about 625 g (1¼ lb) plain flour

1 Steep the saffron in the hot water for 5 minutes.
2 Heat the milk, pour off a little to cool to lukewarm and prove the dried yeast in it, if using.
3 Add the butter, sugar and salt to the rest of the milk. Stir in the saffron and proved yeast. Mix the easy-blend yeast into the flour.
4 Add half the flour to the milk and beat well with a wooden spoon. Add the remainder gradually to make a shiny, cohesive dough.
5 Knead the dough for 10 minutes, until smooth and elastic. Put the dough in a lightly oiled bowl, cover with clingfilm or a cloth. Leave to rise until it has doubled in bulk – about 1½–2 hours.
6 Knock back, and form the dough into a loaf. Put the dough into a 1 kg (2 lb) buttered loaf tin, and leave to rise until it almost reaches the top.
7 Bake in a preheated oven at 220°C, 425°F, gas 7 for the first 10 minutes, then lower the temperature to 180°C, 350°F, gas 4 and bake for a further 15–20 minutes. The loaf should sound hollow when tapped on the bottom.

Banana Bread

75 g (3 oz) butter
125 g (4 oz) sugar
1 egg, beaten
250 g (8 oz) plain flour
2 tsp baking powder
7.5 cm (3 in) vanilla pod
pinch of salt
2 bananas, mashed
75 g (3 oz) raisins

1 Cream the butter and sugar together in a bowl, then add the egg.
2 Sift together the flour and baking powder. Scrape the seeds from the vanilla pod and add to the flour with the salt.
3 Add the flour mixture to the butter and sugar alternately with the bananas. Mix in the raisins. Grease a 500 g (1 lb) tin and pour in the mixture.
4 Bake in a preheated oven at 190°C, 375°F, gas 5 for about 30 minutes until the top is golden and a skewer inserted into the loaf comes out clean.

Gingerbread Biscuits

These gingerbread biscuits are very easy to make and popular with children.

150 g (5 oz) honey
75 g (3 oz) soft brown sugar
25 g (1 oz) butter
2 tsp ground ginger
pinch of ground cinnamon
pinch of ground cloves
pinch of ground black pepper
½ tsp ground cardamom
375 g (13 oz) plain flour
1 egg yolk
1 tsp bicarbonate of soda
50 g (2 oz) icing sugar, sifted
5 ml (1 tsp) lemon juice

1 Heat the honey, sugar and butter in a heavy-based pan, stirring until the mixture is smooth and the sugar has dissolved. Stir in the spices and then leave to cool.
2 Sift two-thirds of the flour into a bowl and add the egg yolk and honey mixture. Mix well. Dissolve the bicarbonate of soda in a spoonful of warm water and add to the mixture. Knead in enough of the remaining flour to make a firm mixture that comes away from the sides of the bowl.
3 Roll out the gingerbread dough on a floured surface until about 1 cm (½ in) thick. Cut out shapes with biscuit cutters or animal or gingerbread figures. Place on a greased floured baking sheet.
4 Bake in a preheated oven at 160°C, 325°F, gas 3 for 10–12 minutes. Mix the icing sugar and lemon juice together with 5 ml (1 tsp) warm water. Use to ice the cooled biscuits.

Chocolate Macaroons

75 g (3 oz) plain chocolate
125 g (4 oz) sugar
150 g (5 oz) ground almonds
½ vanilla pod
¾ tsp ground cinnamon
2 egg whites

1 Melt the chocolate in a bowl over a pan of hot water. Remove from the heat and stir in the remaining ingredients to make a soft paste. A food processor will achieve a good texture quickly.
2 Line a baking sheet with edible rice paper or baking parchment. Roll the mixture into small balls and place them on the sheet. Flatten the tops with a knife.
3 Bake in a preheated oven at 180°C, 350°F, gas 4 for 12–15 minutes until almost firm to the touch. Leave to cool on the paper, then break off the excess rice paper or peel off the baking parchment (if the macaroons stick, wipe the underside with a wet cloth).

Anise Shortbread

125 g (4 oz) butter
40 g (1½ oz) granulated sugar
25 g (1 oz) icing sugar, sifted
250 g (8 oz) plain flour
1 tsp ground anise
¼ tsp salt
10 ml (2 tsp) orange flower water
pine nuts (optional)

1 Cream the butter in a bowl, then add the granulated sugar and icing sugar and beat again.
2 Sift the flour with the anise and salt. Work the flour into the butter mixture, a little at a time, alternating with the orange flower water until a smooth dough is formed.
3 Divide the dough into four or five pieces, then shape into bars or rounds about 8 mm (⅓ in) thick. Put pine nuts on the top if wished, pressing them in slightly with your finger. Place the shortbread on ungreased baking sheets.
4 Bake in a preheated oven at 150°C, 300°F, gas 2 for 15–20 minutes until pale golden, not brown. Leave to cool on the sheets, then transfer to a rack.

VARIATIONS
◆ Other spices can be used instead of anise. Cinnamon, vanilla, cardamom, saffron and safflower all make excellent shortbread.

Cinnamon Biscuits

300 g (10 oz) plain flour
2 tsp ground cinnamon
1 tsp baking powder
150 g (5 oz) soft brown sugar
75 g (3 oz) butter
1 egg
50 g (2 oz) golden syrup
blanched almonds or sesame seeds (optional)

1 Sift the flour, cinnamon and baking powder into a bowl and stir in the sugar.
2 Cut the butter into small cubes and rub it into the flour with your fingertips until the mixture looks like breadcrumbs.
3 Beat the egg, add the golden syrup and beat until smooth. Make a well in the centre of the flour mixture and pour in the egg and syrup.
4 Mix the dough to a smooth ball. Wrap in clingfilm and chill for 30 minutes.
5 Roll out the dough on a lightly floured surface to 5 mm (¼ in) thick. Cut into rounds or shapes. If you wish, decorate the biscuits with blanched almonds or sesame seeds, or leave plain and ice them after baking.
6 Bake in a preheated oven, 160°C, 325°F, gas 3 for 8–10 minutes until golden brown. Cool on a rack.

Chocolate macaroons with vanilla and cinnamon.

Sauces & preserves

Indonesian Soy Relish

An easy relish to accompany satay or even just a bowl of rice.

45 ml (3 tbsp) oil
1 small onion, chopped finely
2 cloves garlic, crushed
½ tsp sambal oelek (pp. 74–5) or chilli powder
salt
90 ml (6 tbsp) dark soy sauce
45 ml (3 tbsp) vinegar
2 tsp sugar
2 kaffir lime leaves or ¼ tsp ground lemon grass
30–45 ml (2–3 tbsp) water

1 Heat the oil in a pan and fry the onion until golden brown. Add the garlic, then all the remaining ingredients and cook for 3–4 minutes, stirring well.
2 Taste and adjust the seasoning if necessary. Remove the lime leaves and serve.

Peanut Sauce

An excellent Indonesian sauce that accompanies satay, rice or vegetables. The recipe may seem to make a large amount, but it usually disappears fast, and leftovers keep well. Thinned with coconut milk or with water, it can be used as a sauce for Gado Gado (p. 134).

30 ml (2 tbsp) sunflower or groundnut oil
½ tsp ground coriander
2 tsp ground cumin
1 tsp ground ginger
a few curry leaves
1 tsp trassi, crumbled (optional, pp. 154–5)
1 kg (2 lb) large onions, finely chopped
350 g (12 oz) peanut butter
60 ml (4 tbsp) coconut cream
1 tbsp sambal oelek (pp. 74–5, or available from Oriental stores)

1 Heat the oil, add the dry spices, curry leaves, trassi and onions. Stir well, put a heat diffuser under the pan and turn the heat as low as possible. Add the peanut butter and coconut cream.
2 Cover and cook for several hours, stirring occasionally to ensure that the mixture does not stick. It should make enough liquid of its own to prevent this, but if necessary add 15–30 ml (1–2 tbsp) water.
3 Eventually the sauce will become thick and smooth when stirred vigorously – you can speed this up by using a food processor, but the sauce will be inferior to one produced by long, slow cooking.

4 Remove the curry leaves and add the sambal, but do not cook for more than another hour or so because the taste of sambal gets hotter and hotter as it cooks.

Romesco Sauce

This versatile sauce comes from the province of Tarragona in Spain. The name derives from the romesco pepper, an aromatic, mildly hot *capsicum annuum*, that is almost impossible to find outside Spain. Alternatively, use a fresh red pepper and a pinch of cayenne. The sauce is usually served with fish or shellfish, but also goes well with boiled vegetables and vegetable salads. It makes a good spread for bread too.

1 dried romesco pepper or 1 fresh red pepper and a pinch of cayenne
4 cloves garlic, unpeeled
175 g (6 oz) tomatoes
10 hazelnuts
10 almonds
sprig of parsley, chopped
30 ml (2 tbsp) wine vinegar
75 ml (3 fl oz) olive oil
salt and pepper

1 Remove the seeds from the romesco pepper and soak the pepper in water for 30 minutes.
2 Put the fresh pepper, garlic, tomatoes and nuts on a baking sheet. Place in a preheated oven at 200°C, 400°F, gas 6. Remove the nuts after a few minutes when they are lightly toasted, the garlic and tomatoes when soft and the pepper when the skin has blistered and looks withered – it will take about 25 minutes.
3 Peel all the vegetables. Drain the romesco pepper, if used.
4 Pound or process the garlic and pepper with the nuts. Add the tomatoes and parsley and blend well. Beat in the vinegar and oil as if making mayonnaise. Season with salt and pepper to taste.
5 Leave to stand at room temperature for at least 2 hours before serving.

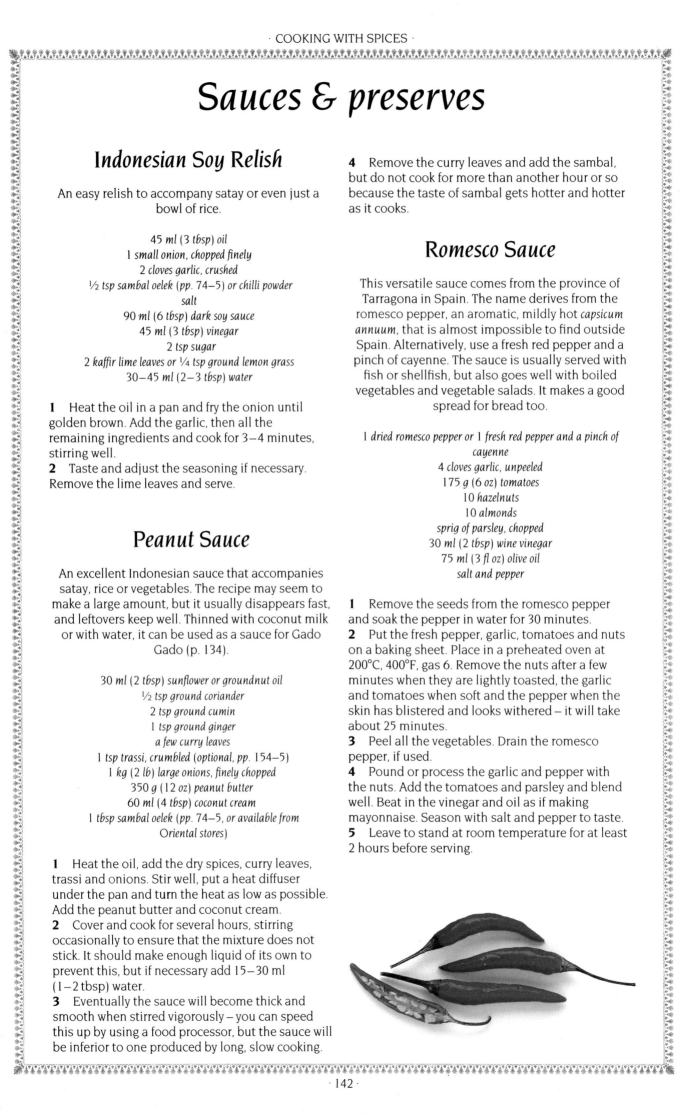

American Cucumber Pickles

MAKES ABOUT 2 KG (4 LB)

1.5 kg (3 lb) cucumbers thickly sliced (ridge cucumbers if possible)
4 large onions, thickly sliced
75 g (3 oz) coarse salt
crushed ice
900 ml (1½ pints) cider vinegar
1 tsp ground turmeric
1 tbsp mustard seeds
1 tsp celery seeds
½ tsp black peppercorns
6 cloves
750 g (1½ lb) sugar

1   Put the cucumbers and onions in a large bowl with the salt and ice. Put a plate and weight on top to press them and leave for 3–4 hours.
2   Bring the vinegar, spices and sugar to the boil, stirring to dissolve the sugar. Take off the heat.
3   Drain the cucumber and onion thoroughly. Bring the spiced vinegar syrup to the boil again and add the vegetables. When the pan comes to the boil again, turn off the heat.
4   Put the pickles into warmed preserving jars. Cover and keep for 2 weeks before using.

Black Olives with Fennel and Allspice

MAKES ABOUT 500 G (1 LB)

500 g (1 lb) black olives in brine
1 tbsp fennel seeds
1 tbsp allspice, crushed
3 bay leaves
olive oil

1   Drain and rinse the olives. Put them into a large jar, sprinkling the layers with the spices.
2   Tuck in the bay leaves, then pour over enough olive oil to cover the olives completely. Store in a cool place for 3–4 weeks before using.

Green Olives with Coriander

MAKES ABOUT 500 G (1 LB)

500 g (1 lb) green olives in brine
4 large cloves garlic
1 tbsp coriander seeds, crushed
½ lemon, sliced
olive oil

1   Drain and rinse the olives. Crack them by hitting with a mallet or rolling pin. Transfer the olives to a large jar, interspersed with the garlic, coriander and lemon slices.
2   Cover with olive oil. Store for at least 3 weeks before using.

Garlic Pickle

MAKES ABOUT 250 G (8 OZ)

The flavour of the garlic mellows pleasantly over time and, after 3–4 months, if there is any left, it can be crushed to add to vegetable and meat dishes.

250 g (8 oz) garlic
1 tbsp salt
3 tbsp fennel seeds
1 tbsp black peppercorns or long pepper
1 tbsp garam masala (pp. 84–5)
1 tbsp nigella
1 tsp chilli powder
¼ tsp ground asafoetida
900 ml–1.2 litres (1½–2 pints) sunflower oil

1   Peel the garlic and check that it is free from blemishes.
2   Put the whole cloves together with the salt and spices into a preserving jar. Cover with oil and put on the lid.
3   Place the jar in a warm place – on the boiler or in the sun if it is hot enough. Stir a few times a day for 5 days. Leave for at least a week, still in a warm place, before using.

Lime Pickle

MAKES ABOUT 300 ML (½ PINT)

6 limes
50 g (2 oz) salt
1 tbsp mustard seeds
1 tsp fenugreek seeds
seeds from 2 star anise
4 small green chillies
125 g (4 oz) brown sugar
1 tbsp ground ginger
45–60 ml (3–4 tbsp) water

1   Cut the limes into quarters. Put them in a wide, flat bowl and sprinkle the salt over them. Leave until next morning.
2   Heat the mustard seeds, fenugreek, star anise and chillies in a dry frying pan. Cover with a lid because the seeds will sputter. When the sputtering subsides, remove from the heat and put aside.
3   Strain the liquid from the limes into a pan. Add the sugar, ginger and the water and boil until the sugar dissolves. Leave to cool.
4   Put the limes and the roasted spices into a preserving jar, mixing them well. Pour the cooled sugar mixture over the limes. Cover and keep for 4 weeks before using.

Tomato Chutney

MAKES ABOUT 1.25 KG (2½ LB)

1.5 kg (3 lb) ripe tomatoes, peeled and chopped
2 large onions, chopped
4 cloves garlic, sliced
175 ml (6 fl oz) white vinegar
1 tsp salt
¼ tsp paprika
¼ tsp ground cloves
¼ tsp ground mace
¼ tsp ground cardamom
250 g (8 oz) sugar

1 Cook the tomatoes, onions and garlic in a heavy pan until reduced to a thick pulp.
2 Stir in half the vinegar, the salt and spices. Bring to the boil and cook to a jam-like consistency.
3 Dissolve the sugar in the remaining vinegar and add to the pan. Cook steadily, stirring frequently for about 15 minutes. The chutney should be very thick. Pour into preserving jars while hot.

Apricot and Apple Chutney

MAKES ABOUT 1.5 KG (3 LB)

500 g (1 lb) dried apricots, chopped
2 green apples, peeled and chopped
3 large onions, sliced
125 g (4 oz) raisins
450 ml (¾ pint) white vinegar
250 g (8 oz) brown sugar
½ tsp mustard seeds
¼ tsp ground ginger
½ tsp ground allspice
1½ tsp salt

1 If they are very dry, soak the apricots for a few hours in a bowl of water, then drain and proceed with the recipe.
2 Put all the ingredients into a preserving pan and cook gently to a thick pulp – it will take about 45 minutes. Stir frequently to prevent sticking. Pour into jars while hot.

Spiced Blackberry Jelly

MAKES ABOUT 1 KG (2 LB)

1.5 kg (3 lb) blackberries
300 ml (½ pint) water
¼ tsp grated nutmeg
¼ tsp ground cinnamon
pinch of ground cloves
sugar
juice of 2 lemons

1 Put the blackberries into a preserving pan with the water and spices. Bring to the boil and cook steadily for 30 minutes until all the juice is extracted. Stir and press the fruit occasionally.
2 Strain through a jelly bag. Measure the juice and for each 600 ml (1 pint), add 500 g (1 lb) sugar.
3 Put the blackberry juice, sugar and lemon juice into the preserving pan and cook gently until setting point is reached. Pour into jars while hot.

Green Walnut Preserve

MAKES ABOUT 750 G (1½ LB)

This unusual preserve comes from Greece. It is rather time-consuming but well worth making if you have a supply of green walnuts.

1 kg (2 lb) green walnuts
1 kg (2 lb) sugar
1 litre (1¾ pints) water
juice of 3 lemons
12 cloves

1 Wear rubber gloves while preparing the walnuts or your hands will be badly stained. Peel off the outer skin – a potato peeler works well – and soak the nuts in cold water for 6–7 days, changing the water twice a day. This will draw off any bitterness.
2 In a stainless steel or enamelled pan, boil the sugar, water and lemon juice to make a thick syrup.
3 Drain the nuts and add to the syrup with the cloves. Simmer for 40 minutes, then remove the pan from the heat and leave to cool.
4 Make sure the nuts are submerged in the syrup, put a plate on top if necessary. Leave for 48 hours.
5 Remove the walnuts and bring the syrup to the boil again, then simmer for a further 40 minutes.
6 Pour the walnuts and syrup into warmed preserving jars, cool and close.

Preserved Plums

MAKES ABOUT 1 KG (2 LB)

1 kg (2 lb) small firm plums
175 g (6 oz) sugar
300 ml (½ pint) wine vinegar
2 pieces cassia bark
½ tsp cloves
3–4 blades of mace

1 Soak the fruit in cold water for 10 minutes. Drain and prick each one a few times with a needle. Put the plums into preserving jars.
2 Put the sugar, vinegar and spices into a pan and bring to the boil. When the sugar has dissolved, continue to simmer for 4–5 minutes, then cool.
3 Pour the spiced mixture over the plums, distributing the spices evenly. Make sure that all the plums are covered by the liquid.
4 Cover and keep for 10 days before using.

VARIATIONS

◆ Apricots may be prepared in the same way, so may larger fruits such as peaches or pears, but they should be quartered and pears should be peeled.

Drinks

Spiced Tea

SERVES 4—6

1 litre (1¾ pints) water
1 cinnamon stick
3 cloves
3 allspice berries
3 cardamoms, crushed
15 ml (1 tbsp) black tea

1 Simmer the water and spices for 5 minutes.
2 Bring to the boil and pour on to the tea in a warmed tea pot. Infuse for 5 minutes.

Mexican Coffee

SERVES 4—6

In Mexico, the coffee is made in the earthenware mugs in which it is served, but it can be made in a saucepan or coffee pot.

½ cinnamon stick
4 tsp dark brown sugar
900 ml (1½ pints) water
60 ml (4 tbsp) coarsely ground dark roasted coffee

1 Heat the cinnamon, sugar and water slowly until the sugar has dissolved.
2 Stir in the coffee, bring to the boil and remove from the heat. Bring to the boil again, remove from the heat and leave to infuse for 1—2 minutes. Strain and serve.

Spiced Ayran

SERVES 4

A refreshing drink that is widely served in Turkey.

450 ml (¾ pint) natural yogurt
450 ml (¾ pint) cold water
seeds from 8 cardamom pods
ice cubes (optional)

1 Whisk the yogurt until creamy, then whisk in the water, a little at a time.
2 When the drink is well blended, stir in the cardamom seeds. Serve at room temperature or over ice cubes.

Chilli Vodka

Infuse 2 *red chillies* in a *bottle of vodka* for 24 hours. Strain and keep the vodka in the freezer. It is very good for head colds.

Caribbean Ginger Beer

MAKES ABOUT 4.8 LITRES (8 PINTS)

250 g (8 oz) fresh ginger, peeled
2 limes, thinly sliced
15 g (½ oz) cream of tartar
1 kg (2 lb) sugar
4.8 litres (8 pints) water
1 tbsp dried yeast

1 Grate the ginger into a large bowl or jar, then add the lime slices, cream of tartar and sugar.
2 Warm a cupful of the water, sprinkle over the yeast and leave to prove.
3 Boil the rest of the water and pour over the ginger and sugar mixture. When this has cooled to lukewarm, whisk the yeast to a paste and stir it in.
4 Cover and leave to stand for 2 days. Strain and bottle. The ginger beer will keep for up to a week in the refrigerator, otherwise for 2—3 days.

Mulled Wine

MAKES ABOUT 750 ML (1¼ PINTS)

150 ml (¼ pint) water
1 small piece of cinnamon stick
1 small piece of dried ginger, bruised
8 cloves
a few pieces of orange zest (optional)
75 g (3 oz) sugar
1 bottle red wine

1 Bring the water to the boil in a pan with the spices, orange zest and sugar to make a thick syrup.
2 Pour in the wine and heat almost to boiling point, then serve.

Clove Cordial

"Take of bruised cloves and cassia buds a quarter of an ounce each, and a dozen Jamaica peppercorns [allspice]. Infuse the spices in hot water and keep the bottle by the fire, close stopped, for a night or two. Strain this to three pints of proof spirit, and add syrup to taste. Filter, and colour with burnt sugar, or a bit of cochineal. Mace or nutmeg, bruised, may be added to clove cordial. It is grateful and tonic."

Extract from *The Cook And Housewife's Manual*, Mistress Margaret Dods, 1833 edition.
NOTE: The spirit may be clear eau-de-vie or (as befits a Scottish recipe) whisky. It is not necessary to colour it, in my opinion.

5

Spices in the home

In the past, spices played a much wider role in the home than the limited culinary one we assign to them today. As well as flavouring and preserving foods, they freshened the air, warded off unwelcome insects and helped to prevent and cure a wide range of ills. The following pages provide some traditional ideas for using spices as room fresheners. Their medical applications are examined, and detailed instructions are provided for the best ways of preparing and storing spices in the home.

Spiced delights

" I'll choose a small orange as round as the moon is,
That ripened its cheek in the sunniest grove,
And when it is dry as a midsummer hayfield
I'll stick it all round with the head of a clove."

Eleanor Farjeon, *The Clove Orange*

THESE DAYS we associate spices primarily with cooking, but their fragrance has long been important to sweeten the air, and they were even thought to ward off the plague and other diseases with their alleged antiseptic properties. Sweet-smelling herbs were strewn on the floor, spice balls carried in the hand or hung from a belt, lavender bags and bundles of herbs put into cupboards and drawers, bowls of pot-pourri used to freshen and scent the air.

By Elizabethan times soaps and disinfectants, lotions and ointments, tinctures and cordials, mouthwashes and medicines were made in the home from flowers and herbs from the garden and drugs and spices from the apothecary or grocer. Early receipt books usually had as many instructions for these still-room preparations as for food. The following recipe for *Aqua composita* is a typical example.

Aqua composita

" Take *a gallon* of *Gascoign wine*, of *ginger, galingale, cinnamon, nutmegs* and *graines* [of paradise], *annis seeds, fennell seeds,* and *carroway seeds*, of each *a dram*; of *sage, mints, red roses, thyme, pellitory, rosemary, wild thyme, camomile, lavender*, of each *a handful*, bray [crush] the spices small, and bruise the herbs, letting them macerate 12 houres, stirring it now & then, then distil by limbecke of pewter [in a pewter still] keeping the first cleare water that commeth, by it selfe, and so likewise the second. You shall draw much about a pinte of the better sort from everie gallon of wine."

From *Delights for Ladies*, Sir Hugh Plat, 1602

Aqua composita and similar waters such as *aqua mirabilis*, cinnamon water, and aniseed water were taken for all sorts of ailments - heartburn, melancholy, loss of memory, to aid digestion and "to comfort the heart". At least they probably had a tonic effect on the sufferer.

Distilling spiced waters and making soaps and mouthwashes may no longer be practical domestic activities, but it is agreeable and easy to make pot-pourri, clove oranges and other spice and herb bags to scent your rooms and cupboards, and to keep out moths and other insects.

Essential oils, distilled from plants, provide an easy way to impart aroma, but because they are volatile and rapidly lose their fragrance, a fixing agent is needed to absorb and hold the oil. In the past animal fixatives such as musk were common, but now vegetable fixatives, usually orris root and gum benzoin, are the norm. Vanilla pods, cinnamon sticks and cloves are also effective fixatives.

A *sweet rose bag*

" Cut the white part from some scented rose petals. Let them dry thoroughly, then mix with a few drops of rose oil and ground cloves. Fill small bags to put in your drawers."

From *The Compleat Confectioner*, Hannah Glasse, 1760

Rosemary and verbena bags

a handful of dried rosemary flowers
a handful of dried lemon verbena leaves
25 g (1 oz) ground orris root
grated dried rind of 1 orange
½ nutmeg, grated

Mix all the ingredients together and use to fill small cotton or muslin bags.

Sweet bag to perfume linens

" *½ cup dried rosebuds*
⅓ cup ground orris root
1 cup coriander seeds, bruised in mortar
1 tsp ground cinnamon
10 slightly bruised whole cloves
½ cup dried orange flowers
½ tsp common salt

Mix well and fill small cotton bags."

From *Potpourris and other Fragrant Delights*, Jacqueline Hériteau, 1975

Moth bags

Moths were a bane in many households and a variety of scented mixtures was developed to deter the insects from laying their eggs amongst fabrics and clothes. Here is a recipe based on one in *The Practical Housewife*, 1860.

1 Mix together equal amounts of *ground caraway, cloves, nutmeg, mace, cinnamon* and *tonka beans*.
2 Add as much *ground orris root* as the total amount of spices, mix well and put into little bags.

A *clove orange*

Choose a thin-skinned orange, score it in quarters and tie a ribbon around it, leaving a length to hang it by. Make holes with a darning needle or bodkin before proceeding to stick the fruit full of cloves or you will end up with several broken stalks and get sore fingers. Arrange the cloves so that the heads are touching. Mix together equal quantities of orris root powder and ground allspice or cinnamon and roll the orange in it so that it is coated with the powder. Wrap it in tissue paper and leave it for two weeks. With time the pomander will dry out completely and get smaller, but it will keep its fragrance for a year or two.

Traditional pot-pourri

1 litre (1¾ pints) dried fragrant leaves and flowers
200 g (7 oz) coarse salt
50 g (2 oz) ground cloves
50 g (2 oz) ground allspice
75 g (3 oz) ground benzoin
75 g (3 oz) ground orris root
50 g (2 oz) brown sugar
a few small pieces of cinnamon
45 ml (3 tbsp) brandy

1 Choose an assortment of sweet-smelling sprigs and flowers from the following selection: *rose petals, lavender, scented geranium, rosemary, lemon balm, marjoram, bay leaves*, and make sure they are thoroughly dry. Put them in a bowl and mix with 150 g (5 oz) of the salt. Leave for 3-4 days.
2 Mix the remaining salt with the dry ground ingredients and sugar, and add to the pot-pourri with the bits of cinnamon. Transfer the mixture to a jar with a lid and sprinkle over the brandy. Mix well and keep tightly covered when not in use. Stir it occasionally, and if the pot-pourri dries out add a little more brandy.

Eleanour Sinclair Rohde's pot-pourri

" 1 litre (1¾ pints) rose petals
175 g (6 oz) coarse salt
3 tbsp allspice, bruised
3 sticks cinnamon, bruised
1½ tbsp cloves, bruised
3 nutmegs, crushed coarsely
1 tbsp anise
50 g (2 oz) lavender flowers
25 g (1 oz) ground orris root
5 ml (1 tsp) oil of jasmine
3 drops each oil of rose geranium, lavender, lemon
2 drops oil of neroli
1 drop oil of patchouli
1 drop oil of rosemary

Gather rose petals in dry weather, and dry in shade by spreading out well on paper. Damask roses are best. When quite dry make in a covered crock, one handful of salt to three of rose leaves. Let it remain five days, turning twice a day. Then add allspice and cinnamon. Let it remain a week, turning from bottom to top. Then add everything else, including oils. You can add fresh dried leaves of marjoram, sweet balm, verbena, tuber rose, orange blossom, gardenia, clove carnation, violets, etc. Stir with a wooden spoon at intervals."

From *Gardens of Delight*, Eleanour Sinclair Rohde, 1934

Floral pot-pourri

The word "leaves" here means petals as well as sweet-scented leaves. For bay salt use sea salt.

" Take a large quantity of *rose-leaves* and dry them in the house, not out of doors because the air is inclined to take the scent away. Add sweet-scented *geranium, verbena, honeysuckle*, and *lavender*. Sprinkle the leaves with *powdered cloves*, a large tablespoonful of *bay salt, musk, oil of lavender, oil of cinnamon, oil of cloves*, and mix these ingredients well together."

From *A Book of Scents and Dishes* by Dorothy Allhusen, 1926

Pomanders & pot-pourris

Most pot-pourri blends contain a number of aromatics among their ingredients. Spices such as cloves and vanilla impart their own sweet, warming fragrance as well as helping to retain the scents of aromatic oils. Secured in a fabric bag, a blend of spices is an effective way of scenting clothes in storage and protecting them from insects. Another traditional air-freshener is the clove orange.

SWEET BAGS

Rosemary and lemon verbena (recipe, p.148).

Moth bag spice mix (recipe, p.149).

Sweet bag to perfume linens (recipe, p.148).

CLOVE ORANGE

An orange stuck with cloves keeps its fragrance for a year or two (p.149).

POT-POURRI BLENDS

Eleanour Sinclair Rohde's pot-pourri (recipe, p.149).

Traditional pot-pourri (recipe, p.149).

Floral pot-pourri (recipe, p.149).

POT-POURRI BOX

An attractive way of displaying pot-pourri.

Spices as medicines

ALTHOUGH SPICES are little used in Western medicine today, they are still widely prescribed in China and in Indian Ayurvedic medicine, much as they were thousands of years ago. Cassia, ginger, cardamom, pepper, sesame and poppy have perhaps the oldest history of medicinal use in the East; in the ancient civilizations of Mesopotamia, the seed spices - dill, anise, caraway, fennel - were more common. The Egyptians, Greeks and Romans all used large numbers of medicinal plants, both local and Oriental. Seven of the 37 volumes of Pliny's *Natural History*, written in the first century AD, were devoted to medicinal plants. The Arabs, for centuries at the centre of the spice trade, drew on much of the knowledge left by the Greeks as well as the wealth of medical learning that came from the East. This was brought to the West by the writings of Avicenna, a leading physician in 11th-century Arabia.

The demand for spices in Europe was as much for their medicinal applications as for their culinary appeal. The pepperers and spicers who sold them later became the apothecaries who dispensed medicines. For centuries, the population of Europe suffered from plagues and epidemics. Many believed that these were spread by foul air, and spices became popular as air purifiers. People took to carrying balls of aromatic spice blends, or pomanders, as protection against pestilence and unpleasant odours.

The range of conditions for which spices have been used is extensive and includes treating snakebites, bed-wetting, menstrual problems, poor eyesight, piles, jaundice, indigestion, diabetes, migraines, insomnia and lack of sexual energy. The warming quality of spices such as mustard and cayenne led to their use in the treatment of colds, circulatory problems, and muscular aches and pains. In ancient Greece, mustard was mixed into a plaster form to alleviate lung congestion. The mustard plaster was thought to warm the skin and open the lungs, making breathing easier, although if applied for too long or made too strong, it caused skin blisters. Powdered mustard was added to baths to soothe tired aching feet and to help cure colds by raising the body temperature.

Chillies contain capsaicin, a chemical that increases blood circulation upon contact. The increased flow of blood brings relief to strained muscles, and chillies are common ingredients in muscle liniments. Unbroken chilblains, neuralgia and lumbago are also sometimes treated with ointments containing cayenne.

Another warming spice, ginger, was considered so beneficial by the Chinese that at one time it was planted in pots and carried on long sea voyages so it could be eaten by the crew to prevent scurvy. In contemporary China it is a traditional remedy for colds and coughs, kidney problems and even hangovers. Once introduced to Europe ginger was taken freely for its wide-ranging medical effects and recent research has proved that it stimulates blood circulation, helps in the digestion of fatty foods and prevents travel sickness.

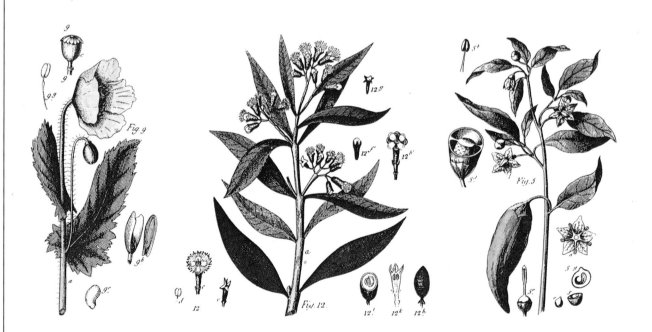

Opium poppy *The plant yields seeds for spicing and a sticky sap - the source of the painkillers opium, morphine and codeine.*

Cloves *Antiseptic and an effective painkiller, cloves are a traditional cure for toothache and nausea.*

Chillies *A source of capsaicin, which improves circulation, chillies also have powerful antibacterial properties.*

The value of spices in aiding digestion has been recognized since ancient times. The Romans used to serve spice cakes at the end of a banquet to help the body digest rich foods, and today a dish including anise, fennel seeds, caraway and dill is often presented at the end of an Indian meal. Other spices known to help digestion include ajowan, cassia, celery seeds, chillies, cumin, fenugreek, ginger, mustard and pepper. Dill water is a traditional cure for hiccups and colic in babies.

Recent research has shown that cinnamon, used in ancient Egypt in embalming mixtures, is effective against bacterial and fungal infection. Anise is another spice with antibacterial properties, although its main use today is as a flavouring in cough medicines and as a carminative. Cloves, long recognized as a toothache cure, are antiseptic and have a mild anaesthetic effect if chewed whole or rubbed on the gums. Clove tea is a traditional remedy for nausea and indigestion.

Spices as essential oils

Ancient cultures valued aromatic plant oils not only for their healing properties, but also as perfumes, anointing oils and preservatives. In the days of the Muslim Empire (7th to 11th centuries), Arab scientists perfected the art of distillation,

developing techniques to extract the essential oils from aromatic plants. Cinnamon and cloves were two of the earliest spices from which they distilled the essential oil, although the most renowned was the costly attar of roses. The Crusaders and their followers brought the knowledge of distillation to Europe and by the 14th-century the apothecaries' guilds were established, their members supplying oils, ointments and infusions to the public.

Today many essential spice oils are distilled in producing, as well as importing, countries. It is a time-consuming, expensive operation requiring very large quantities of the best raw materials in order to extract a minute amount of oil. Pure essential oils are therefore costly. Some oils have been copied synthetically, but only the aroma is reproduced, not the therapeutic properties. Synthetic oils can be used in the cosmetic and food industries, but not for any healing process.

An important use of essential oils today is in the science of aromatherapy, a modern, holistic version of an old healing art, intended to strengthen the body's self-defence mechanisms against disease. The oils are applied through massage, baths and inhalations; some have a calming effect, others stimulate the body. Of the spice oils, cinnamon, juniper and clove are the most important for aromatherapy.

Inside an apothecary's shop Spices and herbs were ground together in different combinations and prescribed to treat a wide range of ills.

Preparing & storing spices

Selecting spices

Spices come in many forms, from seeds and powders to fresh roots and aromatic leaves. When buying dried berries, fruits and seeds, always choose whole spices as these keep their flavour and aroma much longer than powdered forms, and can be ground easily as required. Ready-ground spices may be adulterated; if you grind your own you can be sure about their content. When selecting dried spices check that they are a good colour, not faded, and that they do not smell musty. Avoid fruits and pods that look cracked, shrivelled or hollow, and bags of seeds that contain a lot of powder and dust. Fresh galangal, ginger and lemon grass have a cleaner taste than the dried versions, and are better for some dishes.

How to store spices

Fresh spices: Lemon grass, screwpine, curry leaves and kaffir lime leaves will keep for a week or so when fresh if stored in the salad drawer of the refrigerator. Try putting the leaves in a sealed plastic bag with a little moisture and air to prevent them wilting. Galangal, ginger and chillies will keep for 2-3 weeks in the refrigerator. Ginger and galangal may benefit from being wrapped in kitchen paper to absorb any moisture that can cause rot. Lemon grass, chillies and leaves can also be frozen for up to six months. An alternative method for keeping fresh ginger for several months is to peel, slice and bottle it in sherry.

Dried spices: Store in airtight containers in a cool, dry cupboard as direct light, heat and moisture impair their quality. Whole spices will keep for several months, even up to a year, if stored in this way. However, most ground spices fade in colour and taste within a few months. When unsure how long your spices have been stored for, check if they smell musty, or if their aroma is faint, in which case they should be replaced.

Other spices: Mustard can be stored both ready-made and in powdered form for up to a year. Some spices such as dried tamarind and vanilla pods can be stored for several years.

Preparing spices

Detailed information about the best ways of preparing each spice is provided in the Spice Index (pp.18-67). Here are some general instructions on basic techniques referred to throughout the book.

Grinding: Spices are crushed or ground to release their flavour and aroma. With a few exceptions such as dried ginger, mace, turmeric, cassia and cinnamon, whole spices are easy to grind. Grind them as you need them rather than in advance, so that the full flavour is preserved. The traditional

Indian method is to pound them with a large pestle against a block of stone with a recess in it. Japanese mortars, which have ridged bowls, are good for pulverizing chillies and garlic when making pastes. Some spices, such as allspice, coriander and fenugreek, will grind down successfully in a pepper mill. A quicker method is to use a coffee grinder, either electric or hand-operated. I keep a separate grinder for this purpose. A food processor also comes into its own for making pastes and purées, although you need to grind a relatively large quantity for the blades to work effectively.

Bruising: Rather than being ground to a powder, some spices such as dried ginger, juniper berries, and cardamom pods are just slightly crushed to release their flavour. Either press lightly with a pestle in a mortar or place the spices in a bag or envelope and tap them with a rolling pin.

Dry roasting: This process heightens the flavour and aroma of such spices as coriander, cumin, fagara, fenugreek, mustard seeds, nigella, poppy seeds and sesame seeds, and is considered essential in Indian cookery. Heat a heavy frying pan and after 2-3 minutes, put in the whole spices. Dry roast over a medium heat for several minutes, stirring or shaking the pan frequently to prevent the spices burning. Continue roasting until the spices turn dark brown and give off a heady, fragrant aroma - this should take about 5 minutes. Remove the spices from the heat and allow to cool in a dry bowl before grinding them to a powder.

Some special points & ingredients

A few spices require special handling, which is described on the relevant pages in the Spice Index (pp.18-67). Here is additional advice for preparing specific spices and some unusual ingredients commonly used in spice recipes from Asia.

Black salt: An aromatic, rather unsalty condiment that is sold in Indian grocery shops. A smaller quantity of ordinary salt may be used as a substitute when required in spice mixtures.

Chillies: Be careful when handling chillies. It can help to wear a pair of rubber household gloves, especially if there is a lot of preparation involved. If you need to remove the seeds from a chilli before using it in a recipe, it is easier to do so before chopping it. For a fresh chilli, cut it in half and scrape out the seeds using the point of a knife. With a dried chilli, cut off the stalk end with a knife or a pair of scissors and shake out the seeds.

Coconut milk: An essential ingredient in Indonesian cuisine which can be made from fresh, desiccated or creamed coconut. It is easiest to use creamed coconut, which is sold in firm white blocks. To make 175 ml (6 fl oz) thick coconut milk, dissolve 75 g (3 oz) chopped creamed coconut in 175 ml (6 fl oz) hot water; for thin milk, use only 25 g (1 oz) coconut. The milk can be kept for 24 hours in the refrigerator; if it separates, stir well before use.

Garlic: Crushed garlic is a common ingredient in a lot of spice mixtures. A quick and effective way of crushing garlic is to place an unpeeled clove on a work surface and press down on it with the heel of your hand on the flat blade of a large knife. The garlic skin will work loose. To crush further, pound the clove in a mortar with a few grains of salt.

Ginger: To use fresh ginger, first remove the skin with a sharp knife and then either slice, chop or grate it with a fine grater. Ginger is easier to chop if it is first crushed with the flat side of a knife to separate the fibres.

Trassi: A firm paste made of rotted shrimps that is used widely in Southeast Asian cookery. It has an extremely pungent smell similar to a meat extract and can be bought in packets in Oriental grocers, sometimes under the Malay name *blachan*. To heat trassi, wrap it in foil and grill it until it darkens, or put it in a preheated oven at 180°C, 350°F, gas 4 for a few minutes.

Alternative names for spices

Some of the more unusual spices can only be bought in Indian, Chinese or Southeast Asian shops. The spices are often not labelled with their English name; this list should help identify them.

Names are given according to the type of shop in which they can be useful. The Southeast Asian names are indicated by country: Indonesia (I); Malaysia (M) and Thailand (T).

SPICE	INDIAN	CHINESE	SOUTHEAST ASIAN
ajowan	ajwain, carom, lovage		
anise	saunf	yan kok	jintan manis (M)
asafoetida	hing		
caraway	kala jeera, shia jeera		
cardamom	elaichi	wok lok wuat	kapulaga (I); buah pelaga (M); (luk) kravan (T)
cassia buds	nagkesar		
cayenne / chilli powder	lal mirch		pisi hui (T)
coriander	dhania		ketumbar (I,M); pak chi met (T)
cubeb			tjabé djawa (I)
cumin	jeera		jinten (I); jinten putih (M); yee raa (T)
cumin, black	kala jeera		
curry leaves	kari patta		daun kari (I); daun kai pla (M); bai karee (T)
dill	sowa		adas cina (I)
fennel	saunf	wooi heung	adas (I,M)
fenugreek	methi		
galangal, greater			laos (I); lengkuas (M); khaa (T)
galangal, lesser		sa leung geung	kencur (I)
kaffir lime leaves			daun jeruk purut (I); bai makrut (T)
lemon grass			sereh (I,M); ta krai (T)
mace			bunga pala (M); dawk chand (T)
mango powder	amchoor		
mustard seeds	rai		biji sawi (M)
nigella	kala jeera, kalonji		
pomegranate	anardana		
poppy seeds	khas khas		kas kas (M)
saffron	kesar		kunyit kering (M)
screwpine	rampe		daun pandan (I); bai toey hom (T)
sesame	til	chee ma	bijan (M); dee la (T)
star anise		pak kok	bunga lawang (I,M); poy kak bua (T)
tamarind	imli		asam (I); asam java (M); mak kam (T)
turmeric	haldi	wong geung	kunjit (I,M); kamin (T)
zedoary	amb halad, gandhmul, kachur		kentjur (I)

Index

Page numbers in **bold** refer to entries in the Spice Index.

Bibliography & Acknowledgments

Allhusen, D: A Book of Scents and Dishes, London, 1926

Apicius: De Re Coquinaria, trans Flower and Rosenbaum as The Roman Cookery Book, London, 1958

Arctander, S: Perfume and Flavouring Materials of Natural Origin, New Jersey, 1960

Beckmann, J: A History of Inventions, Discoveries and Origins, London, 1846

Black, P: The Book of Potpourri, London, 1989

Boxer, C R: The Dutch Seaborne Empire, London, 1965

Braudel, F: The Mediterranean and the Mediterranean World in the Age of Philip II, trans Reynolds, London, 1972

Braudel, F: Structures of Everyday Life, trans Reynolds, London, 1981

Braudel, F: The Wheels of Commerce, trans Reynolds, London, 1983

Brennan, J: Thai Cooking, London, 1981

Brissenden, R: South East Asian Food, London, 1969

Browne, P: The Civil and Natural History of Jamaica, London, 1755

Burkill, I H: Dictionary of the Economic Products of the Malay Peninsula, Kuala Lumpur, 1966

Clair, C: Of Herbs and Spices, London, 1961

Cobbett, A: The English Housekeeper, London, n.d.

Cost, B: Asian Ingredients, London, 1990

David, E: A Book of Mediterranean Food, London, 1950

David, E: Spices, Salt and Aromatics in the English Kitchen, London, 1970

Delaveau, P: Les Epices, Paris, 1987

Diaz, B: The Conquest of New Spain, trans Cohen, London, 1963

Gerard, J: The Herball, London, 1633 edition

Glasse, H: The Art of Cookery Made Plain and Easy, London, 1747

Glasse, H: The Compleat Confectioner, London, 1760

Goldstein, D: A Taste of Russia, London, 1985

Greenberg, S and Ortiz, E L: The Spice of Life, London, 1983

Grieve, M: A Modern Herbal, London, 1931

Grigson, J: Jane Grigson's Fruit Book, London, 1982

Guinaudeau, Z: Fez Vu Par Sa Cuisine, Rabat, 1966

Halıcı, N: Nevin Halıcı's Turkish Cookbook, London, 1989

Harrison, Masefield, Wallis: The Oxford Book of Food Plants, Oxford, 1969

Hemphill, R: The Penguin Book of Herbs and Spices, London, 1968

Hériteau, J: Potpourris and Other Fragrant Delights, London, 1975

Jaffrey, M: An Invitation to Indian Cooking, London, 1976

Jump, M: Cooking with Chillies, London, 1989

Kennedy, D: The Art of Mexican Cooking, New York, 1989

Khawam, R: La Cuisine Arabe, Paris, 1970

Kitchiner, W: The Cook's Oracle, London, 1817

Landry, R: Les Soleils de la Cuisine, Paris, 1967

La Varenne: Le Cuisinier François, Paris, 1651

Law's Grocer's Manual, London, 1950 edition

Leipoldt, C L: Leipoldt's Cape Cookery, Cape Town, 1975

Lowenfeld, C and Back, P: The Complete Book of Herbs and Spices, Newton Abbot, 1974

Luke, H: The Tenth Muse, London, 1962

Masselman, G: The Cradle of Colonialism, London, 1963

McCormick: Spices of the World Cookbook, New York, 1964

Meilink-Roelofsz, M A P: Asian Trade and European Influence, The Hague, 1962

Le Ménagier de Paris, 1393, trans Power as The Goodman of Paris, London, 1928

Monardes, N: Joyfull Newes out of the New-found Worlde, trans Frampton, London, 1596

Morrison, S E: Journals and Other Documents on the Life and Voyages of Christopher Columbus, New York, 1963

Nola, R de: El Libro de Guisados, Manjares y Potajes, Logroño, 1529

Nott, J: The Cook's and Confectioner's Dictionary, London, 1726

Odarty, B: A Safari of African Cooking, Detroit, 1976

Origo, I: The Merchant of Prato, London, 1963

Orta, G da: Colloquies on the Simples and Drugs of India, trans Markham, London, 1913

Ortiz, E L: The Best of Caribbean Cooking, London, 1975

Owen, S: Indonesian Food and Cooking, London, 1986

Parkinson, J: Theatrum Botanicum, London, 1640

Parkinson, J: Paradisi in Sole, London, 1656 edition

Parry, J H: The Spanish Seaborne Empire, London, 1974

Parry, J W: The Spice Handbook, New York, 1945

Pigafeta, A: Magellan's Voyage around the World, trans Robertson, Ohio, 1906

Pires, T: Suma Oriental, 2 vols, trans Cortesão, London, 1944

Plat, H: Delights for Ladies, London, 1602

Polo, M: The Travels, trans Latham, London, 1958

Pruthi, J S: Spices and Condiments, New Delhi, 1976

Purseglove, J W; Brown, E G; Green, C L; Robbins, S R J: Spices, 2 vols, London, 1981

Redgrove, H S: Spices and Condiments, London, 1933

Roden, C: A New Book of Middle Eastern Food, London, 1985

Rohde, E S: Gardens of Delight, London, 1934

Rosengarten, F: The Book of Spices, Pennsylvania, 1969

Sahni, J: Classic Indian Cooking, London, 1986

Sahni, J: Classic Indian Vegetarian Cooking, London, 1987

Scappi, B: Opera dell'Arte del Cucinare, Venice, 1570

Schafer, E H: The Golden Peaches of Samarkand, Berkeley, 1963

Silva Gameiro, E da: A Viagem de Vasco da Gama, Lisbon, 1972

Smires, L B: La Cuisine Marocaine, Paris, 1971

Stobart, T: Herbs, Spices and Flavourings, London, 1970

Tannahill, R: Food in History, London, 1973

Taw Kritikara, M L and Pimsai Amranand, M R: Modern Thai Cooking, Bangkok, 1977

Tropp, B: The Modern Art of Chinese Cooking, New York, 1982

Tsuji, S: Japanese Cooking, Tokyo, 1980

Universidad Melendez y Pelayo: Conferencias Culinarias, Barcelona, 1981

Vuyk, B: Eet een Beetje Heet, Amsterdam, 1966

Wilson, C A: Food and Drink in Britain, London, 1973

Winter, J M van: Van Soeter Cokene, Bussum, 1976

Author's acknowledgments

The Tropical Products Institute, Kent, The Commonwealth Secretariat and The American Spice Trade Association have been very helpful in answering questions, supplying trade figures and other information.

The Saffron Walden museum and Maria Jose Sevilla of Foods from Spain gave help on saffron production; Jane Grigson on the Rotterdam Museum of Ethnology's exhibition of spices and the spice trade. Alicia Rios, Suzanne Hodgart, Nevin Halıcı, Darra Goldstein and other friends brought spices and information back from their travels. Paul Breman provided recipes and notes on Indonesian food. Marion Burdenuik, Sasha Breman and Elinor Breman tested recipes.

My curiosity and enthusiasm for spices grew from many years of publishing cookery books, and I am grateful to all my authors – and most notably to Elizabeth David – who are indirectly responsible for this book. Those whose work I have drawn on directly are acknowledged in the text.

Carolyn Ryden and Tanya Hines at Dorling Kindersley have been thorough and helpful in their editing, and Sarah Scrutton has been imaginative and painstaking in her design for the book.

Dorling Kindersley would like to thank Jill Somerscales, Barbara Croxford, Laura Harper and Heather Dewhurst for editorial work; Tracey Ward for helping with the design; Hilary Bird for the index; Ruth Carim for help with proofreading; Lyn Rutherford for preparing food for photography; Kew library; the National Spice Bureau; the Indian Spice Information Bureau.

The following people helped to track down and supply spices and props for photography: Kirit Patak at Patak (Spices) Ltd, Wigan, Lancs; Judith and Robert Dahan; L. B. Scrutton; Erol Acarturk.

ILLUSTRATORS
Julia Cobbold: pp. 12tl, 13r, 16bl, 20, 21, 26, 29, 32, 33, 36, 37, 38, 42, 43, 46, 48, 49, 50, 51, 56, 57, 60, 61, 62, 70, 72, 74, 76, 80, 84, 90, 92, 94, 96, 98, 100, 102, 104
Antonia Enthoven: pp. 22, 23, 30, 31, 34, 35, 40, 41, 44, 45, 52, 54, 55, 58, 59

PICTURE CREDITS
All photography by Martin Norris except for:
Anthony Blake: pp. 17t, 18b
The British Library: p. 14t
Peter Chadwick: pp. 18–19, 84–5
E.T. Archive: pp. 11t, 13t, 153
Hulton Picture Library: pp. 12, 15b
Mansell Collection: p. 10
National Spice Bureau: pp. 14r, 15r, 17b

Key: t = top; b = bottom; l = left; r = right